WRITERS INC

SCHOOL TO WORK

SOURCEBOOK

A SourceBook of student writing guidelines,
models, and workshops to accompany

WRITERS INC

SCHOOL TO WORK

WRITE SOURCE

GREAT SOURCE EDUCATION GROUP

a Houghton Mifflin Company
Wilmington, Massachusetts

Before You Begin . . .

It is important for you to know a few things about your *School to Work SourceBook* before you begin to use it.

First of all, your *SourceBook* contains a wonderful selection of narratives and essays written by students and professionals from across the country. You will not find a more interesting and diverse collection of writing under one cover anywhere. To go along with these models, we have included clear, step-by-step guidelines that show you how to develop your own writing. The models stimulate you to write; the guidelines help you to carry out your work.

Second, your *SourceBook* contains a variety of letters, memos, reports, and other forms of workplace writing for you to study and practice. This section of your *SourceBook* should provide you with a number of valuable experiences you can take with you into the workplace.

Third, your *SourceBook* contains a collection of writing workshops covering all aspects of the writing process. The skills and strategies that you practice here will lead to real improvement in your writing.

Finally, your *SourceBook* is designed to be used with the *Writers INC: School to Work* handbook. Whenever you see a reference like this ("Refer to . . .") in a *SourceBook* activity, you are being directed to the handbook for additional help. Together, these two books make quite a team.

Now, take a few minutes to page through your *SourceBook*, section by section. Stop, look, and read as you go. Once you've completed your quick tour, you will be **ready to begin.**

Written and Compiled by

Patrick Sebranek, Dave Kemper, Verne Meyer,
John Van Rys, Laura Bachman, Kathy Henning, and Randy VanderMey

Illustrations by

Kim DeMarco
Cover Illustration by Chris Krenzke

Printed in the United States of America

International Standard Book Number: 0-669-40876-X

5 6 7 8 9 10 -POO- 02 01 00 99 98 97

An Overview of the *School to Work SourceBook*

Part I   The Forms of Writing

The forms of writing section offers a variety of real-life writing experiences. Student and professional models are provided for each form of writing, as are step-by-step guidelines.

Part II   Writing in the Workplace

The writing in the workplace section contains writing activities useful to anyone preparing to enter the world of work.

Part III   Writing Workshops

The writing workshops cover all phases of the writing process—from selecting interesting subjects to organizing writing, from advising in peer groups to editing for clarity.

Part I The Forms of Writing

Personal Writing

Subject Writing

Academic Writing

Persuasive Writing

Part II   Writing in the Workplace

Letter Writing

Writing to Get a Job

Writing on the Job

Part III Writing Workshops

Searching and Selecting

Generating Texts

Developing Texts

Reviewing Texts

Revising Texts

Refining:
Sentence Strengthening

Refining: Editing

Refining: Proofreading

The Forms of Writing

Level 1 Activities and Outcomes

The activities in the level 1 framework provide students with a wide variety of opportunities to re-create and connect past incidents, to describe other people and events, to develop essays and personal responses, and to form explanations and summaries.

Personal Writing:

Reminiscence of School Life ● Bring to life a memorable time from an early year in school.

Reminiscence of a Group ● Share a memory concerning a particular group.

Essay of Experience ● Develop an essay exploring what a personal experience says about you or your society.

Subject Writing:

Character Profile ● Develop an in-depth report about a person.

Extended Experience ● Form a detailed account of a firsthand experience that extended over a period of days.

Observation Report ● Base a report on sensory impressions related to a visit.

Compiled Report ● Draw information from several sources into a focused report.

Academic Writing:

Essay of Definition ● Define a concept using a variety of approaches.

Literary Analysis ● Prepare an analysis of a story, theme, character, etc.

Persuasive Writing:

Ad Script ● Create a script for an ad that could be performed.

Personal Commentary ● Present your observations about the state of the world around you in an interesting, colorful style.

Essay of Argumentation ● Argue convincingly for or against a controversial topic.

Overview of the Forms of Writing

Each form of writing is designed to be efficient and user-friendly for both the teacher and student. Each student-guidelines page is presented in a clear, step-by-step fashion. All models contain an introduction and helpful margin notes.

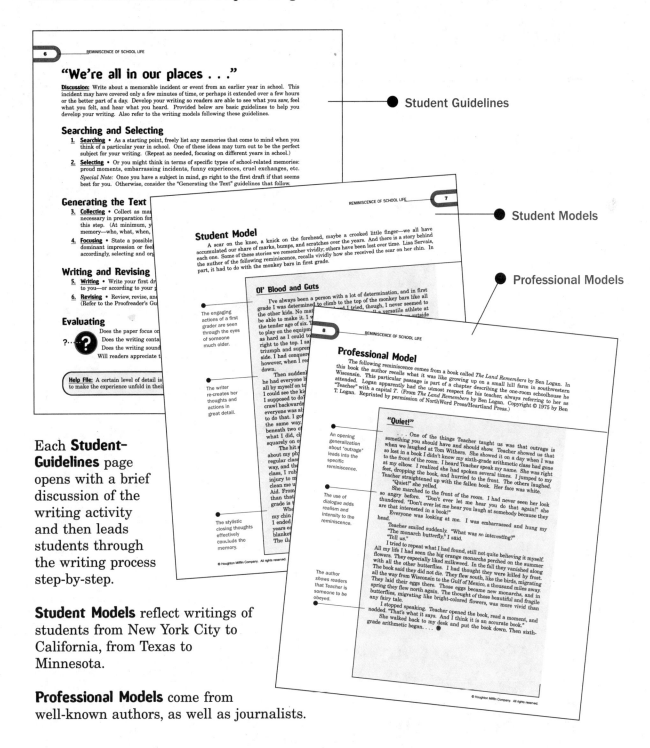

● Student Guidelines

● Student Models

● Professional Models

Each **Student-Guidelines** page opens with a brief discussion of the writing activity and then leads students through the writing process step-by-step.

Student Models reflect writings of students from New York City to California, from Texas to Minnesota.

Professional Models come from well-known authors, as well as journalists.

Personal Writing

"The thought of those beautiful and fragile butter-flies, migrating like bright-colored flowers, was more vivid than any fairy tale."

—Ben Logan

Reminiscence of School Life

When you write about past experiences, you focus on the people and events that were part of those experiences. In the process you gain two things: (1) new insights into yourself and others, and (2) a new appreciation of past experiences.

"We're all in our places . . ."

Discussion: Write about a memorable incident or event from an earlier year in school. This incident may have covered only a few minutes of time, or perhaps it extended over a few hours or the better part of a day. Develop your writing so readers are able to see what you saw, feel what you felt, and hear what you heard. Provided below are basic guidelines to help you develop your writing. Also refer to the writing models following these guidelines.

Searching and Selecting

1. **Searching** • As a starting point, freely list any memories that come to mind when you think of a particular year in school. One of these ideas may turn out to be the perfect subject for your writing. (Repeat as needed, focusing on different years in school.)

2. **Selecting** • Or you might think in terms of specific types of school-related memories: proud moments, embarrassing incidents, funny experiences, cruel exchanges, etc.

    Special Note: Once you have a subject in mind, go right to the first draft if that seems best for you. Otherwise, consider the "Generating the Text" guidelines that follow.

Generating the Text

3. **Collecting** • Collect as many specific details and personal thoughts and feelings as necessary in preparation for your first draft. Listing or free writing will work well for this step. (At minimum, you will want to answer the 5 W's and H related to the memory—who, what, when, where, why, and how.)

4. **Focusing** • State a possible focus for your writing—a sentence (or two) expressing a dominant impression or feeling you want to convey about your subject. Then plan accordingly, selecting and organizing details that support this impression.

Writing and Revising

5. **Writing** • Write your first draft, working in details and ideas as they naturally come to you—or according to your planning and organizing.

6. **Revising** • Review, revise, and refine your writing before sharing it with your readers. (Refer to the Proofreader's Guide when you are ready to proofread your work.)

Evaluating

?····? Does the paper focus on a specific school-related memory?
Does the writing contain effective details, examples, figures of speech, etc.?
Does the writing sound sincere and honest?
Will readers appreciate the treatment of the subject?

Help File: A certain level of detail is necessary to make a memory come alive for readers, to make the experience unfold in their mind's eye. Refer to the models to see how it is done.

Student Model

A scar on the knee, a knick on the forehead, maybe a crooked little finger—we all have accumulated our share of marks, bumps, and scratches over the years. And there is a story behind each one. Some of these stories we remember vividly; others have been lost over time. Lisa Servais, the author of the following reminiscence, recalls vividly how she received the scar on her chin. In part, it had to do with the monkey bars in first grade.

Ol' Blood and Guts

The engaging actions of a first grader are seen through the eyes of someone much older.

I've always been a person with a lot of determination, and in first grade I was determined to climb to the top of the monkey bars like all the other kids. No matter how hard I tried, though, I never seemed to be able to make it. I wasn't what you would call a versatile athlete at the tender age of six. Then one day in gym class, Mr. Tom took us outside to play on the equipment. I headed straight for the monkey bars. I tried as hard as I could to work my way up the bars and finally got myself right to the top. I sat on top of these gleaming steel arcs in an aura of triumph and supreme satisfaction, my legs swinging smartly over the side. I had conquered another mountain. My triumph turned to panic, however, when I realized I had no idea as to how I was supposed to get down.

The writer re-creates her thoughts and actions in great detail.

Then suddenly Mr. Tom announced that gym class was over, and he had everyone line up at the door. Except for me that is. I was stuck all by myself on top of the monkey bars. My panic turned to frenzy when I could see the kids marching back into school without me. So what was I supposed to do? I couldn't slide down the bars because I was afraid to crawl backwards. I couldn't yell for help, even if I had wanted to, because everyone was already passing into the door. But of course, I wasn't about to do that. I got up the monkey bars by myself, and I had to get down the same way. It seemed that my only solution was to drop down beneath two of the bars, a tricky sort of free-form fall. And that's just what I did, closing my eyes, holding my breath, and hitting my chin squarely on one of the bars as I made my descent.

The hit stunned me and my chin hurt, but I wasn't really concerned about my physical condition right at that time. I had to get back to my regular class as fast as I could. First graders follow rules in a serious way, and the first rule of order is to be on time, always. Once I got into class, I rubbed my chin and noticed blood on my hand. I showed my injury to my teacher, Mrs. Getzen, and she took me back to the sink to clean me up. She said the chin just looked skinned and gave me a Band-Aid. From what I could see in the mirror, things looked more serious than that, but I didn't say anything. The second rule of order in first grade is to listen to your teacher.

The stylistic closing thoughts effectively conclude the memory.

When I got home, my mom removed my soggy bandage and said my chin was not "just skinned," and she rushed me to the doctor's office. I ended up getting stitches in the exact same place I had them a few years earlier when I hit the kitchen floor chin first after tripping over my blanket. Six stitches on my chin—a badge of honor, a sign of clumsiness. The thrill of victory, the agony of defeat. I still have the scar. ◉

Professional Model

The following reminiscence comes from a book called *The Land Remembers* by Ben Logan. In this book the author recalls what it was like growing up on a small hill farm in southwestern Wisconsin. This particular passage is part of a chapter describing the one-room schoolhouse he attended. Logan apparently had the utmost respect for his teacher, always referring to her as "Teacher" with a capital *T*. (From *The Land Remembers* by Ben Logan. Copyright © 1975 by Ben T. Logan. Reprinted by permission of NorthWord Press/Heartland Press.)

"Quiet!"

An opening generalization about "outrage" leads into the specific reminiscence.

. . . One of the things Teacher taught us was that outrage is something you should have and should show. Teacher showed us that when we laughed at Tom Withers. She showed it on a day when I was so lost in a book I didn't know my sixth-grade arithmetic class had gone to the front of the room. I heard Teacher speak my name. She was right at my elbow. I realized she had spoken several times. I jumped to my feet, dropping the book, and hurried to the front. The others laughed. Teacher straightened up with the fallen book. Her face was white.

"Quiet!" she yelled.

The use of dialogue adds realism and intensity to the reminiscence.

She marched to the front of the room. I had never seen her look so angry before. "Don't ever let me hear you do that again!" she thundered. "Don't ever let me hear you laugh at somebody because they are that interested in a book!"

Everyone was looking at me. I was embarrassed and hung my head.

Teacher smiled suddenly. "What was so interesting?"

"The monarch butterfly," I said.

"Tell us."

I tried to repeat what I had found, still not quite believing it myself. All my life I had seen the big orange monarchs perched on the summer flowers. They especially liked milkweed. In the fall they vanished along with all the other butterflies. I had thought they were killed by frost. The book said they did not die. They flew south, like the birds, migrating all the way from Wisconsin to the Gulf of Mexico, a thousand miles away. They laid their eggs there. Those eggs became new monarchs, and in spring they flew north again. The thought of those beautiful and fragile butterflies, migrating like bright-colored flowers, was more vivid than any fairy tale.

The author *shows* readers that Teacher is someone to be obeyed.

I stopped speaking. Teacher opened the book, read a moment, and nodded. "That's what it says. And I think it is an accurate book."

She walked back to my desk and put the book down. Then sixth-grade arithmetic began. . . . ◉

Professional Model

The following reminiscence tells of a school-related experience in the life of Anne Moody, an African-American woman who grew up in rural Mississippi. The subject of this passage is Ms. Moody's first experience with organized sports. (This excerpt is from *Coming of Age in Mississippi* by Anne Moody. Copyright © 1968 by Anne Moody. Used by permission of Doubleday, a division of Bantam Doubleday Dell Publishing Group, Inc.)

A feeling of fear is established in the opening paragraph.

The specific experience is re-created in great detail.

The final sentence captures the writer's feeling.

Coming of Age in Mississippi

We arrived late [for the game]. The other team was already warming up. Once I looked at those girls out there, all the little courage I had managed to muster up was completely gone. These were the biggest girls I had ever seen. They were even larger than the girls that played on our high school team. They looked like grown women.

"These are some mighty big girls," Mrs. Willis commented to us as if we hadn't already noticed them. And I felt my blood stop circulating. "What you all gotta do," she advised us, "is guard them close and if possible get them to foul a lot. Try to keep them from that goal too." Then she looked at me and started to say something but changed her mind when she saw how I was shaking.

The referee blew his whistle, and the girls from both teams went to the center of the court and surrounded him. I found myself standing there too. "All you girls know the rules of the game?" he asked and we nodded yes. "Well, remember you have only five fouls and you are then taken out of the game and you can only bounce the ball three times before it's passed on to the next girl." When the game started, the referee blew his whistle again and passed the ball to one of the girls on my team. She passed the ball to the other forward opposite her and the forward passed it on to me. I was supposed to pass the ball back to her and fall back to play the pivot. But I didn't. I just looked up at the big girl that was guarding me and froze. "Play that ball, Moody!" I heard Mrs. Willis yell. I held the ball up as though I was going to pass it. But again I froze. "If you don't play that ball . . ." I heard Mrs. Willis say. I looked toward the goal and the only thing I could remember was that I was supposed to shoot. I didn't bounce or pass. I ran straight to the goal with the ball held high above my head, and shot it. All the time I was running, the referee was blowing his whistle and the spectators standing around the court were laughing like crazy. Mrs. Willis took me out of the game in the first quarter. We lost. And everyone blamed me and made fun of me all the way back to school. I had enough embarrassment from that game to last me a year. ◉

"She asked us what we wanted. We began to read to her from our order slips. She told us that we would be served at the back counter, which was for Negroes." —Anne Moody

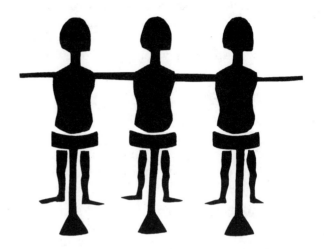

Reminiscence of a Group

In a reminiscence of a group, you focus on an experience that captures the special flavor and dynamics of a certain group. By describing individual members, you show your readers the form and character of the group as a whole.

We're All in This Together

Discussion: Think back to all of the groups you have been associated with. Consider long-term groups like your family and friends as well as short-term groups like teams or clubs. Then re-create a specific memory (experience, incident, etc.) related to one of these groups. Try to capture the group's special flavor by working in specific details that closely and colorfully describe the action as it unfolded. Remember that a reminiscence refers to the past, so think back at least three or four years for a subject. Refer to the guidelines below and the models that follow to help you develop your work.

Searching and Selecting

1. **Searching** • Try to think of a group that has made a strong impression on you, either positively or negatively, momentarily or permanently. Or consider unforgettable experiences that were directly influenced by or related to a particular group. You might also think of the different roles you have played in life (friend, foe, cousin, teammate, organizer, follower, etc.) and list memories related to these roles.

2. **Selecting** • Your goal is to find a group-related reminiscence that you want to explore and share. Once you have a subject in mind, go right to a first draft. If you wish to proceed more carefully, follow the steps listed under "Generating the Text."

Generating the Text

3. **Collecting** • Think about all of the people involved in the memory. What do you remember about them? What were their roles? How did they act? Also think about all of the details of the memory as it unfolded. What happened first, second, and third? What did you see, hear, smell, and feel?

4. **Focusing** • Decide how you would like to present your reminiscence. What dominant feeling or impression would you like to emphasize? Will you need to set the scene with some background information, or will you be able to start right in the middle of the action? Do you need all of the details related to the memory, or can you skip over some of them?

Writing and Revising

5. **Writing** • Develop your first draft freely as details about the group memory come to mind—or according to any planning and organizing you may have done.

6. **Revising** • As you review your first draft, keep in mind your goal of re-creating an experience clearly and colorfully. Have at least one classmate review your work as well. Cut, add, rearrange, and rework your reminiscence accordingly.

Evaluating

?···? Is the writing focused around one particular memory?

Does the special nature of the group come through in the writing?

Has proper attention been given to supporting ideas and details?

Will readers appreciate the treatment of the subject?

Student Model

In this reminiscence, Karen Martinus withholds the setting of her story until halfway through the essay. She minimizes her role in the group, mostly reporting her observations and letting her readers draw their own conclusions. In the closing line, however, she does share a personal lesson.

The Least of These

Consider the significance of the author's use of first names throughout the essay.

Rich told me the same thing every time he saw me. "Duchess is a good dog. She loves me. I take good care of her." I soon discovered that anyone who petted Duchess, or showed any kind of affection toward her, was an automatic friend of Rich. Duchess was the one thing that Rich could count on. On nice days he'd take her outside to sit beneath the trees in the little courtyard; on cold or rainy days the two walked up and down the halls, stopping at many doors to say hi. Although Rich talked about his relatives quite often, I remember only a couple times that they came to see him, or he left to visit them. Instead they sent him money once or twice a month, . . . and Duchess became his family.

Each resident comes to life through well-chosen specific details: Duchess, the mailman uniform, fingernails, etc.

Jack delivered mail every Tuesday, Thursday, and Saturday. Along with the best of the mailmen, he delivered in rain, shine, snow, or sleet. Not that the weather made any difference: he delivered inside. Wearing his mailman uniform (he was a mailman once), he'd hand each person his or her mail. Jack and his wife lived together in one small room, and he'd push her wheelchair wherever she wanted to go—and sometimes even where she didn't. Few of their relatives ever came to visit. Even their children, now grown and on their own, apparently forgot.

Sadie was everyone's baby. She hardly said a word but her face would light up whenever she saw Julie and me. She took great pride in her fingernails, which had been bitten off and were in terrible shape until Julie started cutting, filing, buffing, and painting them twice a week. On her birthday, when she received a balloon from her grandchild, Sadie tied it to her wheelchair and showed everyone. Although she wasn't forgotten by her family, and she was surrounded by rest-home residents— she lived essentially alone.

And then there was Martha. Martha was a talker, talking openly and frequently, usually about her family—where they were all living and what they were doing. She had many pictures of each relative and explained each one in great detail to whoever would listen. She'd get very excited anytime a relative came to visit. Unfortunately, none of her relatives lived nearby, and their visits were few and far between. Although she had many friends, she too was lonely.

The author catalogs four residents, a small sampling of the larger group.

These are only four of the 128 people whom I helped care for last summer at Oasis Rest Home. Medical reasons put Martha and Sadie in the rest home. Rich, on the other hand, was put there because his family no longer could handle the burden of caring for him. However, no matter what their reasons for being in Oasis, these people shared one common need: love. In a world in which love is usually defined as sexy, romantic, and young, people often forget the more basic form—love that lets another person know he's special, needed, and worthwhile. ◉

Student Model

Emily Atkinson, the author of this student model, vividly describes the effects of car travel on her family and, in particular, on her father. Her insights into her "three dads" make this group portrait a delight to read. The author's perceptive description of her father is tempered with love and respect for him. (Reprinted from the June 1992 commemorative issue of the *High School Writer* with permission.)

The reminiscence opens with a generalization about family trips and then focuses on one specific trip.

The father's three personalities are described, using details from this one trip.

The author's general tone in this reminiscence is one of amused but resigned exasperation.

Family Road Trips with My Three Dads

My family has made an art out of family road trips. Since there are five of us, it is too expensive to travel by air. So all of our traveling has been done on the open road. Once, when I was about 11 years old, my father and mother thought it would be great fun to drive from Mississippi, where we lived, to Salt Lake City, Utah, to visit my aunt and uncle. Yes, I said drive. Two weeks cramped in a van with the people I was so lucky to be related to. We were asked to make several educational stops at the Grand Canyon and other national parks famous for tourists carrying cameras and wearing Bermuda shorts and calf-length tube socks. As a veteran of these family excursions, I have found there are actually three personalities rolling around inside my father that only appear on family trips.

First, there is the Gung Ho father. This father usually lasts the first 200 miles. He is so overjoyed, one can see the fireworks popping in his head. On our trip to Utah, this father lasted an exceptionally long time—all the way to Louisiana. He talked about all the exciting and profound things we would learn from seeing the Grand Canyon with its awe-inspiring beauty and its gigantic size. He popped in a tape of family favorites. Uh, favorites when we were about five, that is. My father's voice boomed as he sang a little off key, but who could bear to tell him? You see, my father is vulnerable; and I don't think he could understand that his roaring family enthusiasm can be devastating to a preteen. I could only be thankful we were not in public when he had these outbursts.

When we crossed over the Louisiana state line, my father was pushing 70 miles per hour and singing at the top of his lungs. We, of course, were plugged into our headphones, which blasted more recent tunes. When the highway patrolman pulled my father over, we were all stunned. The officer promptly wrote a $60 ticket and handed it to Dad. Meanwhile, the man was transforming into the second kind of father. This is the one I affectionately call the Bear. The Bear fell silent after the ticket-issuing and snapped off the tape player. No more did the old familiar songs pour from his lips. What flew from his lips then was probably not repeatable. I could not hear the exact words, but by the creases in his forehead and the low, even voice that sounded like it was coming through clenched teeth, I could tell that the monster had emerged from the boiling furnace of my father's brain. The Bear can also crawl out on such occasions as having car trouble or getting lost.

However, in situations like the two just mentioned, my father can turn into the Male Ego more often than the Bear. We experienced this father twice on the trip to Utah, once when we were lost while trying to find my aunt's house. This kind of father delves back into his college days and feels all the glory of a proud know-it-all. The moment my father gets lost, it becomes unmentionable that it is his fault. It's the weather, his wife, or his children who have distracted him to the point of missing the correct exit or taking the wrong turn. And everyone in the family understands never to mention the absurd—asking for directions. He is Man. He knows how to find the way. Finally, after rounding the same block 20 times that day, we found the map where my mother had put it for safekeeping—in her overnight bag. That was a glorious 30 minutes. Being lost with the Male Ego is certainly not boring.

When the car was acting up on the way home, the Male Ego returned. But we didn't have to worry. As well as not needing directions to a place he has never been to, this kind of father knows all there is to know about cars. This involves all the things his father, a pro at being the third type of father, has taught him about how to change a tire, the oil, and filters. The Male Ego also has a certain instinct about the car being in need of service. Usually, it just feels good to this kind of dad to check around in the engine and look professional for his children's and wife's benefit. So, after doing just that, my father got back into the car and turned on the radio, saying that everything was fine. Hence, the Gung Ho dad emerged once more.

The author moves beyond the Utah trip and describes how she's gone from tolerating to admiring her father's personality quirks.

Since that Utah trip, we have gone to other places, have moved twice (which was a treat with our three cats), and have gone to the beach two summers in a row now. Each time my sisters mark the trip's success by the number of times that the Bear and the Male Ego appear, or measure the height of embarrassment by the number of times the Gung Ho father comes out. I, too, watch out for the Bear and the Male Ego, but Gung Ho doesn't bother me so much anymore. I guess I've learned to accept good ol' Dad with his enthusiasm for our family. I think that's what really makes our family tick. ◉

Professional Model

In this model, Anne Moody recalls a dramatic experience in which she and a small group of fellow blacks staged a sit-in at a segregated lunch counter during the 1960's. (This excerpt is from *Coming of Age in Mississippi* by Anne Moody. Copyright © 1968 by Anne Moody. Used by permission of Doubleday, a division of Bantam Doubleday Dell Publishing Group, Inc.)

Coming of Age in Mississippi

The writer re-creates her experience in great detail from start to finish.

. . . At exactly 11 A.M., Pearlena, Memphis, and I entered Woolworth's from the rear entrance. We separated as soon as we stepped into the store, and made small purchases from various counters. Pearlena had given Memphis her watch. He was to let us know when it was 11:14. At 11:14 we were to join him near the lunch counter and at exactly 11:15 we were to take seats at it.

Seconds before 11:15 we were occupying three seats at the previously segregated Woolworth's lunch counter. In the beginning the waitresses seemed to ignore us, as if they really didn't know what was going on. Our waitress walked past us a couple of times before she noticed we had started to write our own orders down and realized we wanted service. She asked us what we wanted. We began to read to her from our order slips. She told us that we would be served at the back counter, which was for Negroes.

"We would like to be served here," I said.

The waitress started to repeat what she had said, then stopped in the middle of the sentence. She turned the lights out behind the counter, and she and the other waitresses almost ran to the back of the store, deserting all their white customers. I guess they thought that violence would start immediately after the whites at the counter realized what was going on. There were five or six other people at the counter. A couple of them just got up and walked away. A girl sitting next to me finished her banana split before leaving. A middle-aged white woman who had not yet been served rose from her seat and came over to us. "I'd like to stay here with you," she said, "but my husband is waiting."

The newsmen came in just as she was leaving. They must have discovered what was going on shortly after some of the people began to leave the store. . . .

Each new detail adds suspense and drama to the writing.

I told them that we were all students at Tougaloo College, that we were represented by no particular organization, and that we planned to stay there even after the store closed. "All we want is service," was my reply to one of them. After they had finished probing for about twenty minutes, they were almost ready to leave.

At noon, students from a nearby white high school started pouring in to Woolworth's. When they first saw us they were sort of surprised. They didn't know how to react. A few started to heckle and the newsmen became interested again. Then the white students started chanting all kinds of anti-Negro slogans. We were called a little bit of everything. The rest of the seats except the three we were occupying had been roped off to prevent others from sitting down. A couple of the boys took one end of the rope and made it into a hangman's noose. Several attempts were made to put it around our necks. The crowds grew as more students and adults came in for lunch.

We kept our eyes straight forward and did not look at the crowd except for occasional glances to see what was going on. All of a sudden I saw a face I remembered—the drunkard from the bus station sit-in. My eyes lingered on him just long enough for us to recognize each other. Today he was drunk too, so I don't think he remembered where he had seen me before. He took out a knife, opened it, put it in his pocket, and then began to pace the floor. At this point, I told Memphis and Pearlena what was going on. Memphis suggested that we pray. We bowed our heads, and all hell broke loose. A man rushed forward, threw Memphis from his seat, and slapped my face. Then another man who worked in the store threw me against an adjoining counter.

Down on my knees on the floor, I saw Memphis lying near the lunch counter with blood running out of the corners of his mouth. As he tried to protect his face, the man who'd thrown him down kept kicking him against the head. If he had worn hard-soled shoes instead of sneakers, the first kick probably would have killed Memphis. Finally a man dressed in plain clothes identified himself as a police officer and arrested Memphis and his attacker.

Pearlena had been thrown to the floor. She and I got back on our stools after Memphis was arrested. There were some white Tougaloo teachers in the crowd. They asked Pearlena and me if we wanted to leave. They said that things were getting too rough. We didn't know what to do. While we were trying to make up our minds, we were joined by Joan Trumpauer. Now there were three of us and we were integrated. The crowd began to chant, "Communists, Communists, Communists." Some old man in the crowd ordered the students to take us off the stools. . . .

"Which one should I get first?" a big husky boy said.

"That [one]," the old man said.

The boy lifted Joan from the counter by her waist and carried her out of the store. Simultaneously, I was snatched from my stool by two high school students. I was dragged about thirty feet toward the door by my hair when someone made them turn me loose. As I was getting up off the floor, I saw Joan coming back inside. We started back to the center of the counter to join Pearlena. Lois Chaffee, a white Tougaloo faculty member, was now sitting next to her. . . .

We sat there for three hours taking a beating when the manager decided to close the store because the mob had begun to go wild with stuff from other counters. He begged and begged everyone to leave. But even after fifteen minutes of begging, no one budged. They would not leave until we did. Then Dr. Beittel, the president of Tougaloo College, came running in. He said he had just heard what was happening.

About ninety policemen were standing outside the store; they had been watching the whole thing through the windows, but had not come in to stop the mob or do anything. President Beittel went outside and asked Captain Ray to come and escort us out. The captain refused, stating the manager had to invite him in before he could enter the premises, so Dr. Beittel himself brought us out. He had told the police that they had better protect us after we were outside the store. When we got outside, the policemen formed a single line that blocked the mob from us. However, they were allowed to throw at us everything they had collected. Within ten minutes, we were picked up by Reverend King in his station wagon and taken to the NAACP headquarters on Lynch Street. ◉

Ms. Moody remains objective throughout her writing, letting the actions speak for themselves.

This reminiscence provides a firsthand look at the Black Freedom Movement in action.

"The cold, biting wind was my worst enemy, threatening my very peace of mind with every move I made. Standing there, atop the snow by the now mostly ice-covered hill, I pondered over the multitude of choices which lay before me."
—Benjamin Baker

Essay of Experience

In an essay of experience, you reflect upon an earlier experience or situation that has provided a new perspective on life or taught an important lesson. The focal point in this type of essay is the change an experience has brought about.

Experience is the best teacher.

Discussion: John Stuart Mill once said, "There are many truths of which the full meaning cannot be realized until personal experience has brought it home." Keeping this in mind, write an essay in which you recall an experience that taught you an important lesson or changed the way you view yourself, others, or life in general. Note: The terms "before" and "after" can provide an effective frame for this form of writing. "Before a particular experience, I was . . . , but after this time, I . . . ." Think about personal experiences you've had that fit the before-and-after frame; then read the model essays and study the guidelines below.

Searching and Selecting

1. **Brainstorming** • Sharing your experiences with a partner will trigger possible subjects for each of you. Take turns listing memories without getting into stories or details at this point. Just jot down ideas, one after another—first one of you, then the other. Work off each other's thoughts.

2. **Selecting** • Review your list for potential subjects. Select one that fits the before-and-after test. (See introduction above.)

Generating the Text

3. **Free Writing** • Once you determine the experience you wish to write about, free-write to recapture the exact feelings you had at the time.

4. **Focusing** • You will probably discover the lesson—and the effect it has had on you—in the process of free-writing about the experience. Don't, however, feel you must know exactly where you will end up before you start writing.

Writing and Revising

5. **Writing** • Experiment with different starting points for your essay: giving some background, describing the setting, jumping into the action, or using a flashback. Also consider where in your essay you might work in the lesson. You might tell it first, or weave it into the story, or save it for the conclusion.

    Special Note: If you're a writer who needs a more definite plan, consider the model essays. They all start with an experience and save the lesson until the end.

6. **Reviewing** • If you fear that your essay lacks the feeling of your original free writing, read both aloud to a partner. Take turns helping each other restore the "personality" and "expression" of your free writing to your essay.

7. **Refining** • Proofread and edit your essay carefully, using the Proofreader's Guide in your handbook before completing your final version.

Evaluating

?····**?** Is the experience one that can be captured on paper?

Is sufficient background information provided for the experience?

Does the writing show the reader what happened, rather than simply tell a story?

Is the lesson learned tied into the essay in a natural way?

Student Model

In this essay Emmeline Chen shares an experience that added a new dimension to her understanding of racial stereotyping. It will undoubtedly do the same for you. (Reprinted from *Golden Gater Jr.* [June 29, 1990], which is published by the Center for Integration and Improvement of Journalism at San Francisco State University.)

Eliminating the Lighter Shades of Stereotyping

The writer hooks the reader by describing her parents' puzzling behavior.

During the intermission of my high school's production of *Anything Goes*, which I attended with my parents, I noticed my father was upset. He wanted to leave. My mother, who also seemed upset, agreed.

I had seen the performance, so I followed them as they left.

The reaction of the parents is explained.

In the car I learned the reason for my father's anger: the "Chinamen" in the musical. The "Chinamen" were portrayed as foolish, Christian converts blindly following a missionary, though they possessed a *yen* to gamble.

At first, I considered my father's anger unreasonable. The play was written during the turn of the century, I rationalized. That was how people viewed the Asian culture. They didn't know any better. I realized, however, that a play portraying African-Americans as simpleminded fools with a gambling streak would immediately bring about a negative response. People would be outraged and call school officials. Since the stereotypes were about Asians, not African-Americans, no such reaction occurred. The audience simply accepted the portrayal and enjoyed the show.

By the end of the experience, the writer sees discrimination in a new light.

Some will call me oversensitive. They may point out the many bumbling white characters in different movies and plays. However, these characters are usually foils to make the protagonists seem better by comparison. In *Anything Goes*, the "Chinamen" were the only representatives of the Asian race. Though *Anything Goes* was just a play, I wish that people would be more sensitive to the discrimination of all races and work to eliminate even these lighter shades of stereotypes. ◎

Student Model

Personal experiences often teach us lessons that affect the way we see ourselves and the way others see us. Student writer Benjamin Baker shares a lesson about self-worth in the following essay of experience. Look for details that create a sense of immediacy and bring the writer's experience to life. (Reprinted from the June 1992 commemorative issue of the *High School Writer* with permission.)

The writer re-creates the scene for his readers.

I Looked Down on the Eagles

The cold, biting wind was my worst enemy, threatening my very peace of mind with every move I made. Standing there, atop the snow by the now mostly ice-covered hill, I pondered over the multitude of choices which lay before me. On either side of the hill rose roughly lain staircases made of railroad ties, leading the sledders to the beginning of their end. For years, my little brother would race me down the slow side of the hill, seeing who could get the closest to the ice rink which lay by the riverbank at the bottom of the hill.

Why does the writer spend time describing Matthew? How does the description affect the story?

Matthew, younger by two years, had always been more daring than me. When we were younger, living on our family's southern Minnesota farm, he had been the first to climb the giant hackberry tree out back. He had been the first to climb the stairs to the forbidden hayloft, and to take his new dirt bike over the jumps which Mom had warned us not to build. He had been the first to mount our neighbors' white horse when offered a ride, and of course the first to get hurt. But I respected him and never went where he didn't lead. It was one of those unwritten rules which I never disobeyed, until that cold January day last winter.

The writer uses two terse quotations in the middle of the essay. The first represents the writer's "before." The second catapults the writer to his "after."

He didn't look 15 bundled in his blue jacket with his blond hair peeking out from under his bright red cap. Matt had always been the first, and more often than I'd like to admit, the last to hit the ramps. Yet he stood there beside me that afternoon, staring down in awe at the monument which some brave, or incredibly stupid, soul had erected overnight. It was the ramp of all ramps! Made of solid ice, it stood at least two feet tall at the bottom of the steepest part of the hill. The very sight of it sent visions of pain and agonizing screams echoing through my mind.

"I'll go if you go!" I said, knowing that there was no way I was going near that jump.

He took longer than expected to respond. His young adventurous mind seemed to be going over every part of the jump, the approach, and the solid ice landing area like a doe grooming her newborn fawn. When the silence became unbearable, he made his statement.

"I'm not hitting it." That was all he said. That was all he had to say, nothing more, nothing less.

His fear triggered something in me. An anxiety came over me, one I had never felt before, and have not felt since. For all these years I had been inferior to him. He had had an undocumented control over me. The time had come to bring that all to an end. The consequences of hitting the jump were all too predictable; yet somehow, some way, I had to do it. I had to hit that jump!

Without giving Matt a warning of any kind, I leaped onto my plastic red toboggan and began my descent. The wind seemed stronger and colder than ever now, biting even harder into my already chapped face. The entire hill went silent as all the sledders turned their eyes on me and dropped their jaws to the ground, dumbstruck by my utter stupidity. For a brief moment, my left arm reached for the ground, in order to steer me away from the ramp. But, remembering my inferiority, it quickly returned to its rightful place in the sled. The mountain of ice got closer and closer as chunks of snow flew up from under my sled, pelleting my face, literally blinding me. As I hit the jump, I was struck by a sudden and unexpected jerk. My head flew back like a boxer's speedbag, and my entire body went limp. I felt at that instant like an angel, soaring high above the world, free and at ease with everything, looking down on the eagles. A loud crack echoed through the river valley rudely interrupting my dream, sending abrupt pain shooting through my body like lightning through copper wire. My left arm, the arm that had tried to detour me, slammed into the ground; and my limp body followed, bouncing like a flat football. For the first time in my life, I had taken a risk that Matthew wouldn't take.

For the first time in my life, I was not inferior to him. And for the first time in my life, I had a broken bone. I had snapped both of the bones in my left forearm. Was this the superiority I had been striving for, yet tactfully avoiding all these years, or just incredible stupidity? My arm, of course, answered that it was just stupidity. But deep inside, I knew that I was no longer his inferior, and much to my surprise, had never been. ◉

Tension builds as the writer reveals his thoughts at that time.

The experience is retold in great detail using strong visual description and sensory images.

Professional Model

In this entertaining essay, Robert Fulghum uses "sink gunk" to teach an important lesson about life. He speaks from experience, having handled many different forms of gunk in his life. (From *It Was On Fire When I Lay Down On It* by Robert Fulghum. Copyright © 1988, 1989 by Robert Fulghum. Reprinted by permission of Villard Books, a division of Random House, Inc.)

The writer's friendly tone, humor, and graphic descriptions naturally draw readers into the essay.

By focusing on sink gunk, the writer sets the reader up for the weighty lesson he provides in the end.

"Dinner Dandruff"

AFTER THE DISHES ARE WASHED and the sink rinsed out, there remains in the strainer at the bottom of the sink what I will call, momentarily, some "stuff." A rational, intelligent, objective person would say that this is simply a mixture of food particles too big to go down the drain, composed of bits of protein, carbohydrates, fat, and fiber. Dinner dandruff.

Furthermore, the person might add that not only was the material first sterilized by the high heat of cooking, but further sanitized by going through the detergent and hot water of the dishpan, and rinsed. No problem.

But any teenager who has been dragooned into washing dishes knows this explanation is a lie. That stuff in the bottom of the strainer is toxic waste—deadly poison—a danger to health. In other words, about as icky as icky gets.

One of the very few reasons I had any respect for my mother when I was thirteen was because she would reach into the sink with her bare hands—BARE HANDS—and pick up that lethal gunk and drop it into the garbage. To top that, I saw her reach into the wet garbage bag and fish around in there looking for a lost teaspoon BAREHANDED—a kind of mad courage. She found the spoon in a clump of coffee grounds mixed with scrambled egg remains and the end of the vegetable soup. I almost passed out when she handed it to me to rinse off. No teenager who wanted to live would have touched that without being armed with gloves, a face mask, and stainless-steel tongs.

Once, in school, I came across the French word *ordure*, and when the teacher told me it meant "unspeakable filth" I knew exactly to what it referred. We had it every night. In the bottom of the sink.

When I reported my new word to my mother at dishwashing time, she gave me her my-son-the-idiot look and explained that the dinner I had just eaten was in just about the same condition in my stomach at the moment, rotting, and it hadn't even been washed and rinsed before it went down my drain. If she had given me a choice between that news and being hit across the head with a two-by-four, I would have gone for the board.

I lobbied long and hard for a disposal and an automatic dishwasher, knowing full well that they had been invented so that *nobody* would *ever* have to touch the gunk again.

Never mind what any parent or objective adult might tell me, I knew that the stuff in the sink drainer was lethal and septic. It would give you leprosy, or something worse. If you should ever accidentally touch it, you must never touch any other part of your body with your fingers until you had scalded and soaped and rinsed your hands. Even worse, I knew that the stuff could congeal and mush up and mutate into some living thing that would crawl out of the sink during the night and get loose in the house.

Why not just use rubber gloves, you ask? Oh, come on. Rubber gloves are for sissies. Besides, my mother used her bare hands, remember. My father never came closer than three feet to the sink in his life. My mother said he was lazy. But I knew that he knew what I knew about the gunk.

Once, after dinner, I said to him that I bet Jesus never had to wash dishes and clean the gunk out of the sink. He agreed. It was the only theological discussion we ever had.

My father, however, would take a plunger to the toilet when it was stopped up with even worse stuff. I wouldn't even go in the room when he did it. I didn't want to know.

But now. Now, I am a grown-up. And have been for some time. And I imagine making a speech to a high school graduating class. First, I would ask them, How many of you would like to be an adult, an independent, on-your-own citizen? All would raise their hands with some enthusiasm. And then I would give them this list of things that grown-ups do:

> -clean the sink strainer
> -plunge out the toilet
> -wipe runny noses
> -clean up the floor when the baby throws strained spinach
> -clean ovens and grease traps and roasting pans
> -empty the kitty box and scrape up the dog doo
> -carry out the garbage
> -pump out the bilges
> -bury dead pets when they get run over in the street

The writer creates an imaginary graduation speech to announce that being an adult is not what teenagers imagine.

I'd tell the graduates that when they can do these things, they will be adults. Some of the students might not want to go on at this point. But they may as well face the truth.

It can get even worse than the list suggests. My wife is a doctor, and I won't tell you what she tells me she has to do sometimes. I wish I didn't know. I feel ill at ease sometimes being around someone who does those things. And also proud.

A willingness to do your share of cleaning up the mess is a test. And taking out the garbage of this life is a condition of membership in community.

A more serious tone establishes the real worth and meaning of cleaning up the gunk.

When you are a kid, you feel that if they really loved you, they wouldn't ever ask you to take out the garbage. When you join the ranks of the grown-ups, you take out the garbage because you love them. And by "them" I mean not only your own family, but the family of humankind.

The old cliché holds firm and true.

Being an adult *is* dirty work.

But someone has to do it. ◉

Subject Writing

"He took off his wedding ring and gave it to my grandmother. He told my father to take care of her and the younger children. That was the last his family ever saw of my grandfather."
—Kristin Ammon

Character Profile

To write a character profile, you learn as much as possible about your subject through interviewing, reading, corresponding, and reflecting. Then you present the results of your research in a report that discusses the subject's background and beliefs. Character profiles are written often in school and in the workplace.

Getting to Know You

Discussion: Write a character profile or report about a person you know well, a person you want to know better, or a person you want others to remember. A description of a person relies primarily on your abilities to observe and remember your subject; a character profile depends more on your abilities to discover information about a person's background and beliefs. In your writing, focus on those characteristics that make your subject unique. The guidelines below and the models that follow will help you develop your writing.

Searching and Selecting

1. **Choosing** • You really shouldn't have trouble selecting a subject for your writing. You're looking for someone who interests you and who will also interest your readers. Make sure you have access to plenty of information about this person.

Generating the Text

2. **Noting** • Write nonstop about your subject for at least 10 minutes. Consider what you already know about your subject, what puzzles or interests you about this person, what you hope to find out, and so on. Review this writing, looking for angles to explore, questions to answer, or possible features to highlight in your profile.

3. **Collecting** • Collect as much information as possible about your subject through direct interviews, phone conversations, letters, reading, personal reflection, etc. (See the "Help File" below.)

4. **Focusing** • Decide what it is you want to emphasize about your subject. That is your focus. Plan and organize your writing to support this focus.

Writing and Revising

5. **Writing** • Write your first draft freely, working in details as they come to mind—or according to your planning and organizing.

6. **Revising** • Review, revise, and refine your writing before sharing it with your readers. Make sure that your opening lines catch their attention and introduce the focus of your profile, and that your closing gives them something to think about or remember.

Evaluating

?...?

Is the profile "in focus," highlighting something important about the subject?

Does the profile contain sufficient detail?

Does the writing move smoothly and clearly from beginning to end?

Will readers appreciate the treatment of this subject?

Help File: Make sure that you properly prepare for each interview you conduct. If necessary, make an appointment ahead of time, have specific questions ready to ask, listen carefully, and take abbreviated but careful notes.

Student Model

The following character profile reflects Karina Sang's effort to learn about her Chinese heritage. Her father's stories are Ms. Sang's primary source of information. (This article first appeared in *New Youth Connections: The Magazine Written By and For New York Youth*, November 1991.)

The writer highlights important events in her grandfather's life.

Grandfather's Journey
From China to Santo Domingo

I have often wondered about my Chinese grandfather. He died before I was born, and my family has never really said much about him. Someday I would like to go to China and find what is left of my Chinese family. But for now, I have to be satisfied with the few stories my father has told me.

My grandfather left China for Santo Domingo in 1916 with two relatives. His father had been a wealthy merchant, and two of his sons decided to go in search of new horizons. They settled in the Dominican town of Bonao and opened a restaurant called "Sang Lee Long." Even though it had a Chinese name, the restaurant served Dominican food and was very popular.

My grandfather's name was Luis Sang. He never told anyone in our family his Chinese name. He had gone through an arranged marriage in China and left his wife and two sons behind when he moved to the Dominican Republic. In his new country he married again and had 10 children: 7 daughters and 3 sons. My father was one of them.

Details include the grandfather's interests and personality.

Grandfather's restaurant got most of its business from travelers. But when the old highway that had united the south of the Dominican Republic with the capital closed in late 1959, Bonao was isolated. As a result, my grandfather's restaurant went bankrupt. He stayed home after that and never opened another restaurant.

He Played Dominoes and Drank Rum

Over the years, my grandfather had acquired Dominican customs. He liked to hunt, play dominoes and poker, and drink Dominican rum. He was accepted by the Dominican society.

In 1961, he read newspapers that protested the actions of the country's dictator, Rafael Trujillo. He believed so much in the opposition that he wanted to participate in politics, but he couldn't because he wasn't a citizen.

The writer's need to know about her heritage is contrasted with her father's disinterest.

He suffered a heart attack in 1968. His doctor told him he didn't have much time left, three months at the most. He lived another year doing everything the doctor had forbidden. He ate pork, drank, played poker, and smoked. "He died January 26, 1969," says my father in a proud voice, "but the fruits he left behind are still here and I'm part of them."

My father does not feel a connection to his Chinese heritage. It may be because he was never taught anything about Chinese culture.

Unlike my father, I do feel a connection to my Chinese heritage. I keep asking questions about my grandfather's life and wait for the day I can visit Canton, China, to learn more about him. ◉

Student Model

In the following profile, Kristin Ammon provides a look at a person she has never met, a person she nevertheless has a great deal of respect for. Note that this profile provides facts and details about a specific period of time.

An anecdote about the grandfather highlights the first paragraph.

The fortunes of World War II are closely tied to the grandfather's profile.

A detailed account of the grandfather's final moments with his family concludes the profile.

Heritage of War

My grandfather Christian left his native Germany to work as a chemist in Russia during the Depression. At the beginning of World War II, he returned to Germany. One night, he and several of his old schoolmates got together for a glass of beer at a local *gasthaus*. The war naturally dominated the conversation. During the course of their discussion, my grandfather remarked that the Germans wouldn't be able to win the war because the Russians had such a vast wealth of industrial resources. This was considered a defeatist attitude, so one of his "friends" reported him to the Nazi party. My grandfather was summoned to appear in court. The usual sentence for such an offense was life in a concentration camp. Fortunately, the judge was an old friend of his, so he was acquitted.

In the fall of 1944, my grandfather was drafted by the German militia. Since he was a chemist who had to perform necessary duties during the war, he originally had been exempt from the military. But as the war progressed, all the factories were shut down, and any man who could walk was drafted. At a huge ceremony inside a stadium, thousands of men stood on the playing field, listening to speeches. There were Nazi flags, but no uniforms since the militia wasn't part of the official army. Everyone was forced to swear an oath of allegiance. Anyone who refused would have been shot.

In January of 1945, word came that the Russians were approaching Brieg. The residents made preparations to evacuate the women and children to safer parts of Germany. The day arrived, and military police stood by the evacuation train to make sure that no men boarded. My grandfather helped his wife, his baby son, his little daughter, my father, and their grandmother into the train to go to southern Germany, where they had relatives. He took off his wedding ring and gave it to my grandmother. He told my father to take care of her and the younger children. That was the last his family ever saw of my grandfather. ◉

Professional Model

In the following essay, writer Tony Chapelle profiles movie producer Spike Lee. Please note that this profile focuses on one aspect of Spike Lee's life—his sudden and unexpected rise to fame as a moviemaker. (This excerpt first appeared in the *Black Collegian*; it is reprinted by permission of the author.)

The Movement of Spike Lee

The chips were truly down for Shelton Lee. It was 1981, he had just graduated from Morehouse College, and now he was going to New York University to earn a master's degree and a crack at making hit movies. He was dreaming big, but the pressure was on.

Even his grandmother had chipped in to give him tuition money. But the year before, his ten-minute student film—a spoof of the racist silent movie, *Birth of a Nation*—almost got him kicked out of school.

All of the details in this profile present Lee as an outsider— someone who has beaten the odds.

Less than ten years ago Spike Lee lived this scenario, with expulsion staring him in the face and his back against the wall. Yet, perhaps recalling some fairy-tale finale of his favorite sports team, the New York Knicks, Lee fought back at the buzzer and responded with an achievement akin to banging in a three-point jumper to win the playoffs.

The game winner was his master's thesis film which snared the student category Academy Award.... The acclaim he received for *Joe's Bed-Stuy Barbershop: We Cut Heads*, not to mention that it kept him from flunking out, vindicated him as a young filmmaker.

Lee pulled off another coup when he wrote, acted in, and directed *Do the Right Thing*. His script fictionalized the Howard Beach [New York] murder, keeping just the seminal elements—an African-American man is killed, hostility between African-Americans and Italians, a pizza parlor, and a baseball bat.

The final comment by Lee provides some insight into his character. (February is Black History Month.)

The outsider who seeks neither Black- nor White-decreed respectability, Spike nevertheless has a reputation for producing on time, and on a budget. No one is better at getting movies reviewed by the press, or at promoting his own films. He's controversial at every turn . . . "a Black woman can keep three men on a string" . . . "Black colleges haven't yet sorted out color consciousness" . . . "My Nike commercials, even starring superstar Michael Jordan, don't lead to Black-on-Black crime."

His life is thus more complex or original than any script. When asked for the defining factor that has made him the biggest Black director in a century of moviemaking, Lee offers, "My success was not just me. A lot of people decided that we didn't want our films just shown in the month of February...."

Professional Model

In this model, writer Karen M. Thomas profiles the career of Unita Blackwell, Mississippi's first black woman mayor. The profile was written to honor Ms. Blackwell for winning a $350,000 MacArthur Fellowship. (The following excerpt originally appeared in the *Chicago Tribune*, July 5, 1992. It is reprinted by permission of the *Chicago Tribune*.)

Civil Rights Activist Adds to Her Legacy

The profile begins with a description of Mayor Blackwell in action.

MAYERSVILLE, Miss.—Mayor Unita Blackwell stood in front of the former Baptist church that serves as City Hall in this Mississippi Delta town, watching as several people bent over something she couldn't see from the street.

"I want to know what they're doing over there," she said, her tall frame breaking into full stride before she finished her sentence.

Blackwell, 59, has made it her business to know what goes here. It is her town, a poor farming community of 500 that was incorporated 16 years ago in her living room. She has been mayor ever since, the first black woman mayor in Mississippi.

Crossing the road to the front porch of a nearby home, Blackwell watched as the occupants cleaned fish fresh from the river. They weren't surprised by her appearance. In Mayersville, everyone knows everyone else, waving from cars and porches when they pass.

Ask the townspeople what Blackwell has accomplished, and they point to the sewer and water systems, public housing and paved streets, necessities that she fought to bring to her town.

Background information about the mayor is provided throughout the profile.

They point to the stream of visitors from across the globe— Egyptians, Asians, Europeans and Americans who venture into this rich, fertile land where cotton and poverty reign, creating an impromptu cultural exchange in a place where people never travel far from home.

They point to the mayor herself, the great-granddaughter of slaves and the daughter of sharecroppers, who has spent most of her life along the Mississippi's banks and has an array of credits: 1960's "freedom fighter," twice president of the National Conference of Black Mayors, a master's degree in regional planning, diplomatic missions to China, former co-chair of the Mississippi Democratic Party.

. . . The town, which contains about a dozen streets, fronts on the Mississippi and is bordered by cotton fields already producing foot-high plants. About 80 percent of the residents are African-Americans, and most are either old or very young, the ones in between having been siphoned off by the lack of jobs and the lure of larger cities.

Her only child, Jeremiah, joined the Navy.

Blackwell sees the development of rural towns like Mayersville as the key to solving the problems of the bigger cities.

The mayor's direct comments provide insights into her personality.

"There are a lot of people in the cities who would be in Mayersville, Miss., if they had a job," Blackwell said.

"If you live in Hollywood and everything around you is glamour and people are just dripping with it, you compare yourself to that. Well, you don't have those delusions here. You know that Mr. Sam over there owns the plantation and has exploited your family for years. You learn to create and make things better where you are. You have real hopes."

. . . In 1964 members of the Student Non-Violent Coordinating Committee came South to help blacks to register to vote, and Blackwell began a political journey of her own.

She tried numerous times to register at the courthouse across from City Hall, and was harassed and arrested. She stood on her porch through many nights, watching for the Ku Klux Klan. Crosses were burned in her front yard. A white man who supported civil rights was beaten several yards from her home.

At the same time, activists such as Stokely Carmichael, Shirley MacLaine, Jane Fonda, college students, black and white, famous and unknown, rich and poor, came to stay at her home or to share a meal.

Blackwell learned about Harriet Tubman and Frederick Douglass, history that she was never taught in school.

She learned about the power of government and voting precincts. She learned she had a gift for organizing, and helped to found the Mississippi Freedom Democratic Party, which challenged the seating of an all-white delegation from Mississippi at the 1964 Democratic National Convention.

Fannie Lou Hamer, a civil rights activist in Mississippi, became her friend and mentor, and Blackwell began to seek what was needed in her impoverished Issaquena County—housing, education and jobs.

. . . At City Hall, the town's one full-time employee, Helen Reed, serves as clerk, tax assessor and tax collector.

The thoughts and feelings of people close to the mayor add depth to the writing.

Annie Johnson, a friend who often accompanies Blackwell on speaking engagements, is helping Reed learn how to use a newly purchased computer to speed up processing town bills.

Johnson and Reed have helped Blackwell conduct the town's business since its incorporation.

Each said that they have grown because of their association with the mayor.

"You can't work for the mayor and not better yourself," said Reed, who held a business degree when she started working for Blackwell more than 14 years ago and is now certified as a clerk.

Blackwell credits the two women with nurturing her spirit.

"They prayed with me and stuck with me. They surrounded me with their strength," she said. "Sometimes you get so low inside. Sometimes people say, 'Child, that's never going to happen here.' But you got to just keep going." ◉

" 'The bees swarmed all around you. You were worried you'd breathe them in. They'd get into your mouth, ears, eyes, nose. You'd feel them all over you.' " —Marilyn Johnson and Sasha Nyary

Extended Experience

When writing an extended experience, you focus on a series of related events that took place recently. Generally, you highlight the important sights, sounds, and feelings rather than sort through the meaning of these events. In the workplace, this type of writing is often used in project reports.

Hey, it's a long story . . .

Discussion: Learning to drive a car, playing in a state basketball tournament, or getting used to a new job are all extended experiences. Each one consists of individual events (like learning to parallel park), but you think of the events as a unit (learning to drive). Choose an extended experience (taking place over a period of days, weeks, or months) from your recent past to write about in a report. (Or plan to write about an experience coming up—a week in algebra class, a weekend trip, etc.) You don't have time for a complete play-by-play account in your report, but you can give an overview and describe the key moments in detail. The guidelines below and the models that follow will help you develop your writing.

Searching and Selecting

1. **Brainstorming** • Have you recently recovered from an injury? Are you rehearsing for a play, struggling in or enjoying a particular class, dating a new boyfriend or girlfriend? Consider these types of experiences when selecting a subject for your report.

2. **Selecting** • If you can't think of a subject from your recent past, plan to report on a specific upcoming experience. Keep a log or journal of this time, noting specific events, activities, observations, thoughts, and feelings.

Generating the Text

3. **Collecting** • Write freely about this period of time to uncover details and feelings. Or generate a list of information about the extended experience (place, time, participants, feelings, etc.). Talk with other people involved in the experience.

4. **Focusing** • Review the thoughts and feelings you have collected. Note key ideas and details you would like to feature in your paper. Next, determine the focus of your writing. (Was the extended experience a time of important learning, complete frustration, wild abandon . . . ?) Finally, consider how to organize your material and plan an opening that will hook your readers.

Writing and Revising

5. **Writing** • Develop the first draft of your report, pulling in pieces of information according to your planning and organizing. Or write freely, as ideas come to mind, if that makes more sense to you.

6. **Revising** • Carefully review your first draft. Then have a classmate review it as well. Make sure to find out what your partner likes and dislikes about your work. Revise and refine your writing until you feel it is ready for publication or sharing.

Evaluating

?...?   Is this report based on experiences taking place over a period of time?

Does the writing convey the overall experience as well as highlight important moments?

Is the writing informative and easy to follow?

Student Model

In this model, Jessica Thompson reports on an extended experience (going to state) that wrapped up the season for her basketball team. By highlighting specific moments, Jessica communicates the excitement of the entire event. (This report first appeared in the March 20, 1992, issue of *MHS Today*, the Milton [WI] High School student newspaper.)

Week Went By in a Blur

The opening sentence identifies the experience and sets the tone.

Some call it "March Madness," but for us, the girls' basketball team, it was the icing on the cake! For me everything is a blur, a hubbub of activity that has made the past few weeks fly by. And I mean fly! Looking back on our basketball season, it is finally starting to dawn on me just how successful we were.

Had someone told me in November that we were going to go to state, I wouldn't have believed them. But we did it! Going to state became a reality for us after the sectional games. We had made our dreams come true—we were actually going to state! *State*—the word itself is amazing.

Last week was an indescribable experience, filled with charged emotions and hopes. So what did we do during our four days in Madison? Well, it all began Wednesday when we left at 6:45 a.m. for the UW Field House. At 8:25 a.m. we took the floor for 25 minutes of practice. Some of us kissed the floor, while others of us just kept looking around, trying to get used to the fact that we were in the barn of all barns.

Highlighting various aspects of the experience provides readers with a sense of what this time was like.

Playing on the Field House floor during the practice and the games was like being suspended in midair. Television cameras were not an uncommon sight. And UW-Madison women's basketball coach Mary Murphy even was there to watch all the different schools practice and compete.

Wednesday night we settled into the Sheraton Inn. But before we could do that, we were whisked off to a banquet where we had the "famous lasagna," the first of many pasta dishes during our stay. Later that night we were finally able to relax in the whirlpool and sauna.

Thursday, Friday, and Saturday are literally a blur in my mind. We decided that if we were not eating, we were sleeping. If we were not sleeping, we were showering or lounging around our rooms battling a case of nerves. But behind everything was basketball, practice, the Field House, 7,000 screaming fans, the growing anticipation for our two games, and a large adrenaline rush each time we ran onto the court.

I decided that the whole experience was like going to basketball camp, except we were a family instead of strangers, everything was catering to us, and 1.7 million television viewers were watching the games.

The report closes with recollections about returning to Milton after the tournament.

Overall, the best part of the weekend was the phenomenal support from our community. It was overwhelming. The bus ride into town behind the fire trucks was an experience beyond words. I think we were all a little choked up when people joined the train of honking cars and came out of their houses to wave to us. And the signs and ribbons! All I can say is thanks, everyone. Thanks for the memories. ◉

Student Model

Have you ever lived with another family, perhaps spending the summer with relatives in another state? Do you remember how it felt at first to be an outsider, and how those feelings changed over time? In the following model, Elizabeth Weisenburger shares, through journal entries, some of her experiences as an exchange student living with a host family in Ecuador.

The writer's opening remarks set the scene for the journal entries that follow.

These entries highlight aspects of everyday life with the writer's host family.

Ecuador

On a cold August morning, the stars blanketed the night sky over the pueblo town on the outskirts of Quito, Ecuador. I stood on the street corner, shaking underneath my wool sweater, waiting for my A.F.S. host father to bring around the car so that we could leave for my trip home to my family in Santa Barbara, California. I was not alone, for already many of the townsfolk were out on the streets, selling fruits or heading out for the day's work. As they passed by, they observed me with a strange curiosity, noticing my fair skin and blonde hair. Men whistled and called in my direction. I stood unmoved; I was used to being different. Time was passing slowly, and the sun was starting to rise over the sloping mountains. Growing weary, I grabbed my bag and searched for my journal that I had kept over my two-month stay, hoping to appear busy and pass the time more quickly.

........**June 27, 1991.** The mountains encompassing the modest A.F.S. campsite tower up towards the sky as clouds creep up their green slopes. The sight of it is soothing because at the moment butterflies are fluttering about my stomach as if they were multiplying by the hundreds! I am leaving for Quito tomorrow to meet my host family and I am anxious, facing the unpredictable and the unknown. My head is spinning with questions! How will I greet them? Will they like me?

........**June 28, 1991.** I'm sitting here in my host parents' room watching television. My father has fallen asleep, after watching the soccer game; my mother soon followed. I just arrived and am already unsure of why I am here. I feel so alone. I haven't met my brother or sister yet.

........**July 4, 1991.** I made French toast this morning for my family. It was an American treat and they praised its taste. Afterward we all went to my parents' room, hopped under the bed covers, and watched an old rerun of *Happy Days* dubbed in Spanish. I have never felt such a strength of family unity. I feel as though I have lived with them for ages, the way they treat me as their own.

........**July 12, 1991.** Language charades have become a great asset. The language barrier is a tough wall to climb, and I get easily frustrated, saying foolish things I did not mean to say. I really think it has humbled me, though; I am so grateful when I can finally say what I want and be able to joke.

........**July 17, 1991.** I just arrived home from a large family dinner. I sat silent most of the time at the table, unable to express what I wanted to say in Spanish, able only to make small talk. It is frustrating at times, and I feel so excluded when I am not able to be included in all the conversations. I feel like I'm on the outside of their world looking in.

.........**July 25, 1991.** Walking to the market and home is an adventure in itself. Today as I walked through a very nice residential area, I passed by an Indian woman and her children. They had enormous baskets tied onto their backs. The woman couldn't even look up. I had not noticed that the young boy was carrying something. It was a baby, slung onto his back. None of them had shoes on. I will never forget the boy's eyes as he looked up to me. He was carrying such a heavy burden at such a young age! What kind of life does he have in front of him? I can't do anything for him.

.........**August 1, 1991.** I am beginning to feel as if I belong here more and more each day. Today I bargained at Ipiales, an open market. I got down to the prices my host mother would have paid, which are very low. So, I'm feeling very accomplished in that a *gringo* like me could get such a *ganga*, or bargain, from the natives.

.........**August 5, 1991.** Last night I was invited to a party. The counselors at A.F.S. had said something about "Latin time." It was last night that I discovered what "Latin time" was. People here are very kicked back with time. My Ecuadorian friends told me they would pick me up at 8:00 p.m.; they really meant around "9:30-ish." I was very mad when they came but soon realized that it is completely cultural. The party made up for it. It is amazing how I had the best time of my life with only a little music and dancing. There are so many deep-rooted feelings that go into dancing; I got swept away. Dancing suddenly became a way of socializing and meeting people.

.........**August 16, 1991.** Today I embarked on a trip into a world unknown to me. It was 8:00 a.m. that the old steam train pulled out of the station. The train was overflowing with people, who had their livestock and produce, so we had to board on the tin roof of the train. Four young boys sat next to me. They were dirty but in good humor, and they stared at my belongings with great interest. As we pulled out of the mountains, we stopped at small stations along the way. The open flatlands were scattered with rickety huts on stilts. Young children ran around naked. I promise no longer to complain about my mother's meatloaf after thinking about what these kids have for dinner. . . .

The blank journal that I arrived in Ecuador with had been filled. I closed it and put it in my backpack as my host father drove up and we left for the airport. In many respects, however, that journal will never be closed. ◉

The writer's perceptive thoughts and comments bring the journal entries to life.

Student Model

In this extended experience, your stomach may growl and your pulse may race right along with writer and wrestler Dan Pelikan. Written in the form of a journal or log, this model presents the writer's experience in an important weekend wrestling tournament.

Ready . . . Wrestle!

Friday—This is the last day before the big event. It's a very typical February day, dreary and cold in a wet and biting sort of way. People outside are bundled and bustling around with their faces lowered against the wind. It's a miserable sight, but as I sit in the lunchroom, I try to keep my eyes on the "outside," not just the outside of the building, but also the outside of me and my diet. I'd rather look out the window than at everyone on the inside scoffing down school pizza and chocolate milk. I've got to lose two more pounds before weigh-in tomorrow, so I'm sticking to celery, no water. I'm practically a crazed and drooling maniac by the time the bell rings to go back to class. What a relief. Now there's algebra and humanities, and then I've earned the right to spend the night in the gym, talking with my fellow wrestlers about tomorrow's Claton-Bernard Wrestling Tournament. I know we'll all be nervous, and practicing will be a relief, a way of winding down as much as gearing up. I know we'll all be hungry, and maybe a bit trembly from our self-imposed fasts, but it will be better to be hungry together. It may sound strange, but at least in the company of my teammates there is an unspoken compassion that puts my aching stomach at ease. I just hope I can sleep well tonight . . .

Saturday—Waking up is hard. I'd rather dream I've won the tournament than get up and face the scale. If I'm not on weight, my dreams will be shattered before I've even had a shot. But I'm hopeful. I've been strict and focused, in the gym and at the table. This tournament is one of the three toughest in New York State. I've placed third and fourth last year and the year before. This time I'm going to win!

We travel to the tournament by bus and it takes an eternity, my stomach growling the whole way. Everyone's pretty quiet on the trip, focusing their thoughts on their first match. Sometimes on these big trips, I feel like cranking a boom box and calling for a poker game, but I know that type of behavior would not be welcomed. So we ride along in virtual silence, talking once in a while about strategy.

When we get there, the first ritual is the weigh-in. I go to the bathroom first and then face the scale. My stomach is churning as I step up. The official slides the metal bar along the measuring apparatus, and that says I've made it, barely. YES! We're all given an allowance of one pound for the evening weigh-ins, so we're free to go to the locker room and devour the feasts we've brought with us. I've got a banana, a bottle of Gatorade, and a delicious Nestle bar, white chocolate. The meal is designed to promote quick bursts of energy for my first match, which is to begin in just a few minutes. All our meals are very much alike, except for Mitch's whose mother always sends zucchini bread with

Specific details leading up to the tournament are provided in the opening journal entries.

Note that this extended experience is developed in great detail from start to finish.

There is an as-it-happened quality about the writing ("I've been picked," "I pass," etc.) that makes for interesting reading. Readers naturally want to know what happens next.

him. He claims it's his good-luck food. As nervous and nauseous as I am, I don't think I'd like to be eating green bread.

I've been picked to take first in the tournament. That's an advantage because the chocolate is still pumping me up, and because some of my competitors will assume there must be a reason for my elevated position. I step onto the mat and tell myself to stay focused; the first match is always hardest because you're not fully in the swing of things. But this match is easy—too easy. I finish my opponent off in seconds, pinning him like I do my younger brother, but, of course, my opponent doesn't scream for Mom. I'm glad I'm conserving energy, but I need to sweat off some more weight or I'll never make evening weigh-in. The field narrows and the competition is looking tougher. My second opponent is stronger and more experienced than the last. The match is hard, and we sweat and grapple for the full six minutes, the length of time allotted by the rules. I win this one by points rather than a pin. It couldn't have worked out better—I pass the scale test, leaving sweaty footprints on the evil thing, and then I'm off the hook until tomorrow. Time to hit that rock-hard hotel bed, and maybe dream a bit more of success.

Sunday—The wake-up call comes in at 7:00 a.m. By tonight there will be a new champion at the 155-pound weight class. I'm going to be that person . . . I'm going to be that person . . . There's no weigh-in today. We'll all be rested and full of healthy calories and energy. The competition will be grueling. There'll be shattered ambitions, bad calls. These thoughts don't occur to me one by one but seem to crowd my brain all at once. It's one big, brain-busting, daunting, exhilarating thought—the desire to win.

I have two matches in the morning. The first one is tough, and a scratch for every point. My opponent feels a bit lighter and taller than I am, and he's quick. But my bulk is also an advantage, and though he's quick, he can't do a lot to budge me, especially as we start to sweat and his grip on me keeps slipping. My hand is raised in victory, 5-3 on a reversal near the end of the match. I have to remember not to clench my teeth down on the mouth guard so hard; I'm giving myself a jaw ache that's distracting. Concentrate . . . Concentrate . . .

The writer doesn't focus on the technical aspects of wrestling. Instead, readers experience the tournament on a much more emotional level.

My next opponent steps onto the mat. He's in incredible shape and he's got white-blue eyes I don't like at all. There's a cold determination in those eyes and in those fisting and unfisting hands and in those perfectly toned calves. Head to toe, I hate him. The match is a complete blur. They say semifinals are won by those wrestlers who can actually stop concentrating and instead wrestle on pure instinct. I know that's true now because he's grabbing at me and I'm responding too quickly. We wrestle for a few seconds beyond the final whistle and then, finally, separate. One point for him and three for me. I've advanced to the finals.

I've got five hours before my final match. My parents have driven up to the tournament and they insist on taking me out for a high-carbohydrate lunch. Though I've been starving myself for days, I have a hard time pressing the potatoes and bread into my stomach. All I can think about is the match. All I crave is quiet and isolation so I don't lose my focus. Mom keeps talking about how she's going to make pumpkin pies and spaghetti—my favorites—every day for the next week to make up for my austere training. My dad keeps trying to give me advice. All I hear is, "What you've got to do, son . . ." I love them, but I find company irritating right now. I don't want my attention diverted from what I have to accomplish today. They finally start talking to each other, and I can fade into my own thoughts.

Later, my stomach full, but hurting with unexpected food and uncertainty, I dress for the final match. As I warm up, sweat forms in my palms, and my forearms shake a little. I wish they'd get this over with. We file into the gym, dim and crowded with spectators. One by one, they call our names and put a spotlight on us as we trot to the middle of the mat to shake hands with our opponents. I have this weird thought that my head is going to explode and fill the gym with burning bits of adrenaline if they don't start the matches soon. My opponent looks at me like I'm a lunatic because I'm smiling over that stupid thought.

Finally, it's time for my match, for action. The whistle blows and my opponent takes a shot at my leg—I feel like it's caught in a vise. Instinctively, I force all of my weight down on his head and force my ankle outward. In a few moments, I'm free and allow myself a small breath of relief. I make my move just as the period ends and receive two points for a takedown. My opponent has chosen the neutral position and we start again. Neither he nor I muster any points in the second period. We're down to the final two minutes. The score is two for me, zero for him. I choose the bottom position—all I have to do is stay off my back and not get called for stalling and I'll win. As the period draws to a close, I take a risk and attempt to score. I escape as the match closes, and it's three for me, zero for him. I've won. I can't believe it, but the first thought that comes to me is that I could really go for some pumpkin pie . . .

The final two paragraphs provide an effective summary of the last match, from the nervous moments before it starts to the feeling of joy when it finally ends.

Professional Model

This model is an excerpt of an article written by Marilyn Johnson and Sasha Nyary. The following background information is shared in the opening section of this article. "In 1914, five years after he left the White House, Theodore Roosevelt, his son Kermit and George Cherrie, an ornithologist, became the first white men to descend Brazil's uncharted River of Doubt, so named because no one knew where it went. Roosevelt almost didn't find out. Though fond of 'the strenuous life,' Roosevelt was defeated by the Amazon—plagued by disease, murderous tribes and starvation. He returned prematurely aged, with a bad case of jungle fever. He never regained his health and died five years later." Here they recount the story of Tweed Roosevelt following his great-grandfather's footsteps down the Amazon 78 years later. (Marilyn Johnson, Sasha Nyary, *Life Magazine*. Copyright Time Warner. Reprinted with permission.)

The article highlights significant events and happenings rather than saying everything about the river trip.

The writers blend straight reporting with direct quotations from some of the participants in the experience.

Roosevelts in the Amazon

For the first few days, the trip went smoothly. Tweed remembers: "Minor rapids, pretty, current reasonably fast. Then it got more and more difficult." At the first major rapids they found out how exhausting portaging boats weighing several hundred pounds each could be. At the next rapids—a tricky double set—the boatmen stopped to scout and decided to make camp.

The next day, their camp enveloped in fog, expedition members packed up and shot the rapids. The route was tricky. One of the rafts had to go sideways and backward to get over a large boulder. At the next rapids, one of the boatmen lost control when he slammed into a wave. Another boat almost flipped.

And getting dumped into the water could be deadly. One afternoon the elder of the Indian guides, Oitamina, "climbed a tree, plucked a bird out of its nest, wrung its neck, hung the bleeding bird on the hook of a Hunk Finn fishing pole and caught four huge piranhas," photographer Mark Greenberg says. Everyone on the expedition came down to the riverbank to stare. "Their teeth were as big as dental plates," Clifton recalls. The Indians took the piranhas up to camp, threw them into a pot and boiled them—teeth, guts and all.

Although everyone on the expedition knew that a member of the 1914 group had lost a toe to piranhas, they continued to bathe in the river. "The jungle is a series of trade-offs," Tweed says. "The alternative to piranhas was sweat bees, and frankly, most of us preferred the piranhas." Bees became a constant problem. Tweed remembers: "The bees swarmed all around you. You were worried you'd breathe them in. They'd get into your mouth, ears, eyes, nose. You'd feel them all over you. And even if they don't sting you, in your subconscious you think they will. You just want to get the hell out of there."

At about the midpoint of the trip, after two weeks on the river, the expedition stopped at an Indian village and discovered that gasoline had spilled into the food, ruining much of it. Their radios, which had never worked well, were now not working at all. Haskell and McKnight noted there was a dirt road through the jungle. If anyone wanted to leave, they said, it was O.K. But the trip out could take days, and as if to dramatize the futility of escape, the skeleton of a crashed plane decorated the landscape.

By the next morning everyone had decided to continue, and they set off down the river. "Today most everyone's ankles are swollen from bug bites," Clifton wrote in his journal. "Many have bites on faces and hands. We dropped into the most remote part of the river today and will be in it for at least eight days. Lots of spiders, stinging bees swarming over everything. The waters we passed through today were infested with piranhas. Tartare yelled 'Cobra!' and pointed up above the rafts about four feet over our heads. There sat, ready to fall into the boats, a large poisonous snake."

The next night another frightening snake was found in camp, one the Brazilians call a two-step, because its victim takes two steps and dies.

By now the adventure was wearing thin: the bugs, the vigilance for snakes, alligators, the heat and humidity that drenched everyone even after the sun went down. Clifton wrote in his journal: "The doctor said almost everyone on this expedition has some infection or affliction."

At night everyone turned in early to escape the insects—everyone except Tweed and an assistant, usually Dr. Walden. Night was when Tweed went to work. He'd string up a white sheet between two trees and light it with a halogen lamp. Insects would fly to the sheet "so thick you couldn't see through them. It was my killing grounds." One night he discovered an assassin bug. The bug is a carrier of Chagas' disease, a parasitic infection that has no known cure and can be fatal. After the insect bites its host, parasites multiply in individual cells, which burst after five days to release hundreds more. Tweed didn't tell his companions about the bug; they were jumpy enough.

Working into the early morning hours, he preserved his specimens in alcohol. When he was finished, he and Walden often had a cocktail, mixing grain alcohol with limes and grapefruits picked in the jungle, and they talked about their determination to finish the trip. "If somebody got hurt, or one of the boats was destroyed, I was not going to be evacuated," Tweed recalls. He and Walden agreed that if the expedition came apart, they would take the 1914 maps and continue on foot. ◉

Describing poisonous snakes, assassin bugs, and piranhas helps readers appreciate the danger involved in this journey.

The thoughts and actions of one individual—Tweed Roosevelt—are emphasized throughout the article.

Professional Model

In the following model, writer Maya Angelou reports on her extended experience as a member of the African-American community living in Ghana. (From *All God's Children Need Traveling Shoes* by Maya Angelou. Copyright © 1986 by Maya Angelou. Reprinted by permission of Random House, Inc.)

All God's Children Need Traveling Shoes

In the opening paragraph, Ms. Angelou establishes the context for this writing—being part of a flourishing African nation.

Ghana was flourishing. The National Council of Ghana Women, which included representatives of all the clans, was beginning to prove that centuries-old tribal mistrust could be erased with intelligence and determination. The Cacao Marketing Board reported huge profits from the country's major export. Large shining office buildings rose in the cities and the land was filled with happiness.

People stopped in the street and said to passersby, "Oh, but life is sweet, oh, and the air is cool on my skin like fresh water."

The shared joy was traceable to President Nkrumah, who had encouraged his people to cherish their African personality. His statements were memorized and repeated in the litany of teachers and students: "For too long in our history Africa has spoken through the voice of others. Now what I have called the African Personality in international affairs will have a chance of making its proper impact and will let the world know it through the voices of its sons." When he declared that West Indians and Black Americans were among Africa's great gifts to the world, the immigrant community gleamed with gratitude.

For the first time in our lives, or the lives of our remembered families, we were welcomed by a president. We lived under laws constructed by Blacks, and if we violated those laws we were held responsible by Blacks. For the first time, we could not lay any social unhappiness or personal failure at the door of color prejudice.

We shadowed Nkrumah's every move, and read carefully his speeches, committing the more eloquent passages to memory. We recounted good gossip about him, loving his name, and furiously denied all negative rumors.

The writer highlights important features of this extended experience until "the happy clock stopped running."

Because we were still American individualists, bred in a climate which lauded the independent character in legend and lore, and because we had been so recently owned, we could not be easily possessed again, therefore we tried rather to possess the charismatic leader. His private life belonged to us. When photos of his Egyptian wife appeared in the papers, we scanned her features and form with a scrutiny bordering on the obsessive.

We, the Revolutionist Returnees, danced the High Life at the Lido, throwing our hips from side to side as if we would have no further use for them, or we would sit together over Club beer discussing how we could better serve Ghana, its revolution and President Nkrumah. We lived hard and dizzyingly fast. Time was a clock being wound too tight, and we were furiously trying to be present in each giddy moment.

Then, one day, the springs burst and the happy clock stopped running. There was an attempt on the President's life, and the spirit of Ghana was poisoned by the news. . . . ◎

"When Dave Henderson steps up to home plate, they shout, 'Hendu! Hendu!' When he hits the ball into the bleachers on the first swing, they jump up and down, pounding on each other's shoulders and high-fiving." —Sandra Lampe

Observation Report

When writing an observation report, you take in all the sights, sounds, and smells of a specific location and present them in such a way that the reader can get a real "sense" of the location. Writing short stories in the classroom or site-inspection reports in the workplace requires a similar kind of observation reporting.

Spectator Sport

Discussion: Write an observation report about a specific location of interest that you actually visit, developing your writing as a continuous flow of sensory impressions or as a more traditional essay, incorporating a focus statement and supporting details. Gather details for your report by recording as many sights, sounds, and smells as you can during your visit. Provided below are basic guidelines to help you develop your writing. Also note the model reports following these guidelines.

Searching and Selecting

1. **Reviewing** • The location you select for your writing must appeal to you and to your readers. Also make sure you have ready access to the location.

2. **Brainstorming** • If you have trouble selecting a location, enlist the help of one or more of your classmates. A small group of you could generate ideas together.

Generating the Text

3. **Noting** • Record as many sensory observations as you can for at least 15-30 minutes at the location of your choice. Don't forget to record snippets of any conversations you happen to hear. (Remember to focus all of your attention on recording sensory details. Don't spend time thinking about your observations.)

4. **Taping** • Some of you might want to use a camcorder or tape recorder to help you collect sights and sounds.

5. **Assessing** • Remember that in its most natural form, an observation report presents the sensory details as they were recorded. However, depending on the nature of your observations, you may decide that it is better to establish a focus for your writing and organize supporting details accordingly.

Writing and Revising

6. **Writing** • Write your first draft freely, working in sensory details as they were recorded or according to your planning and organizing.

7. **Refining** • Review, revise, and refine your writing before sharing it with your readers. (Refer to the Proofreader's Guide in the handbook when you are ready to check for grammar and mechanics errors.)

Evaluating

? ....?

Is the report based on a location readers will enjoy "observing"?

Does the writing contain enough specific details so readers can clearly see (hear, smell, etc.) this location?

Does the writing reflect a sincere effort to record a variety of sensory impressions?

Student Model

The model that follows presents Gina Camodeca's observations made during a visit to a laundromat. The writer records a variety of sensations as they occur, but many of the details are focused on one individual.

"Fluff and Fold"

After some general observations, the writer's attention lands directly on a young woman.

The place is buzzing, thumping, whirring. All the seats by the window are taken, the coffee and candy-bar machines are doing overtime, and Geraldo is unfolding some unseemly topic, though we can only see his lips moving. It's too loud to actually hear him. A very young woman, very pregnant, is trying to sort while trying to keep her rambunctious two-year-old from climbing into the dryers. He's got on little combat boots and camouflage pants. His curly hair is matted up with lint he got in it by rolling on the floor, and his blue eyes sparkle defensively every time his mother looks his way. She is pale as china, with long, static-filled blonde hair. Filling a purple jogging suit to capacity, her stomach sticks out in front of her like a backpack strapped in front, and she has to stretch her arms as far as they can reach to carry her laundry basket around the laundromat.

This section gives a wide-angle view of the laundromat with all of its sights, smells, and sounds.

The place is filling up like a stadium on the night of a concert. People are eyeing the woman with the two-year-old because she's got the most machines in use—12 of the double-loaders. Above the smell of fabric softener, drift the smells of pizza and fries and roasted peanuts from the stand out front and, of course, coffee—always strong, thick-smelling coffee from the machine that has buttons for "extra-light" and "extra-sweet." My stomach begins to rumble, and I wonder if I should sneak around the corner for a Big Mac. But I know someone would throw my clothes in a corner and steal my dryers if I left my post for a minute.

Above all the machine sounds, there is the attendant. She always wears a pink, polyester jumpsuit and is always yelling greetings or warnings at the customers. "Don't sit on the dryers; that's what chairs are for!" "Hey, Sal, you doing the laundry today? In the doghouse at home? Haha." "No I ain't got no change. What do I look like, a vending machine?"

The writer returns to the image of the woman and makes her the center of attention.

The pale, pregnant woman begins moving her mountain of laundry from the double-loaders to the dryers. There are people huddled around her like vultures, waiting for the washers to open up behind her. There are others who are trying to race her for the dryers. She just waddles along, overstuffing the dryers she can get. I can't take my eyes off of her; she looks younger than my younger sister who's still in high school. She looks tired. And then her face changes; she's looking past me toward the door, and her face is lit up with something between coyness and anticipation. "I had to use 12 double-loaders and I'm into my second roll of quarters," she says to the space in back of me. And the two-year-old rushes by, yelling "Daddy!" ◉

Professional Model

The passage that follows is from *Invisible Man* by Ralph Ellison. Note that Ellison shapes this piece with a series of sensory impressions experienced by the main character. (From *Invisible Man* by Ralph Ellison. Copyright 1947, 1948, 1952 by Ralph Ellison. Reprinted by permission of Random House, Inc.)

Invisible Man

The character's attention switches from what he sees outside himself, to the sensations he feels inside.

When I emerged, the lights were still there. I lay beneath the slab of glass, feeling deflated. All my limbs seemed amputated. It was very warm. A dim white ceiling stretched far above me. My eyes were swimming with tears. Why, I didn't know. It worried me. I wanted to knock on the glass to attract attention, but I couldn't move. The slightest effort, hardly more than desire, tired me. I lay experiencing the vague processes of my body. I seemed to have lost all sense of proportion. Where did my body end and the crystal and white world begin? Thoughts evaded me, hiding in the vast stretch of clinical whiteness to which I seemed connected only by a scale of receding grays. No sounds beyond the sluggish inner roar of the blood. I couldn't open my eyes. I seemed to exist in some other dimension, utterly alone; until after a while a nurse bent down and forced a warm fluid between my lips. I gagged, swallowed, feeling the fluid course slowly to my vague middle.

Ellison shapes his observations so readers are able to feel what the main character feels.

A huge iridescent bubble seemed to enfold me. Gentle hands moved over me, bringing vague impressions of memory. I was laved with warm liquids, felt gentle hands move through the indefinite limits of my flesh. The sterile and weightless texture of a sheet enfolded me. I felt myself bounce, sail off like a ball thrown over the roof into mist, striking a hidden wall beyond a pile of broken machinery and sailing back. How long it took, I didn't know. But now above the movement of the hands I heard a friendly voice, uttering familiar words to which I could assign no meaning. I listened intensely, aware of the form and movement of sentences and grasping the now subtle rhythmical differences between progressions of sound that questioned and those that made a statement. But still their meanings were lost in the vast whiteness in which I myself was lost. ◉

Professional Model

In an introduction to "Batter UP!" writer Sandra Lampe writes, "I find baseball games incredibly boring." Not so with people watching. The spectators at this Oakland A's game provide ample material for Ms. Lampe's observation report. Note how the sights, smells, and sounds of the baseball game are brought to life, giving readers an opportunity to share in the writer's experience.

Batter UP!

On this glorious Easter Sunday, my husband Mike has dragged me to watch the Oakland A's "battle" the Milwaukee Brewers. "Dragged" because Mike knows I *hate* baseball; while he, on the other hand, lives for the 162 games for which we have season tickets. "Just come to a game," he pleads. "You'll change your mind."

"We have great seats," Mike is quick to point out. From our position above the visiting team dugout and along an aisle, I can observe all the activity, most of which involves the purchase and consumption of food. It reminds me of a colony of ants, scurrying this way and that, each carrying a little morsel—except these energetic creatures are sporting baseball caps. Up and down the aisle they stream, grandmothers clutching cushions and purses the size of shopping bags; little girls hanging onto their mothers' hands, their ponytails swinging with each step; toddlers riding piggyback on the father's shoulders; teenage boys in baggy shorts, their baseball caps worn backwards; women in torn jeans and halter tops, hair flying in the breeze; eight-year-old boys with catcher mitts racing back and forth, each time carrying a different item: a green and gold pennant, a small wooden bat, red licorice shoelaces.

The assortment of food whisking past my eyes is astonishing. Hot dogs (of course), Polish sausage with kraut, individual-sized pizzas, chicken burritos, submarine sandwiches, steak sandwiches, hamburgers, nachos, French fries, peanuts, chocolate-chip cookies, ice-cream sundaes in miniature plastic A's baseball caps and, best of all, pretzels. Warm pretzels, toasted golden glistening with salt and slathered with mustard squeezed out of little plastic tubes. The aroma of freshly made popcorn, sauerkraut, baking pizza and coffee (even cappuccino!) mingles with the lightly acrid odor of spilled beer, the sweetness of freshly cut grass, and the tang of the California landscape itself—a pinch of eucalyptus and bay, a sprinkle of dust, a shake of sea salt from nearby San Francisco Bay—producing a scent that's hard to resist. Vendors saunter up and down the aisles. "Maa-aalts, getchyer chawwww-clit maa-aalts!" "Pee-nuts! Pee-nuts!" By the end of the second inning (A's - 2, Brewers - 0), Mike is standing in line, along with a quarter of the stadium population, at one of thirty food pavilions scattered throughout the park.

Two rows below me, a father and his two young sons are just completing their third trip. He smiles at a woman nearby. "Good thing I don't have season tickets. I'd go bankrupt." Directly below me are two adolescent boys, catcher mitts poised for action.

One bearded gentleman is dressed entirely in green and gold rags, the outfit set off by a whirligig beanie and a huge banner reading "GO

The writer views the scene from a perfect vantage point—"above the visiting team dugout and along an aisle."

Sensory details give the readers a heightened awareness of what Ms. Lampe observed at the game.

Just as her husband yields to the lure of the food vendors, Ms. Lampe yields to the crowd's excitement.

A'S," which he shakes above his head as he sprints up and down the aisles, rags fluttering in the breeze. Men, young and old, slim and paunchy, stripped to the waist and turning a deeper shade of pink as the afternoon progresses, pass me empty handed and return with frothy containers of beer, sloshing a bit as they settle in their seats.

When Dave Henderson steps up to home plate, they shout, "Hendu! Hendu!" When he hits the ball into the bleachers on the first swing, they jump up and down, pounding on each other's shoulders and high-fiving. "This is Henderson's first homer in two years. He's been injured," Mike informs me. Twenty-five thousand people are on their feet, cheering wildly. The noise is deafening, a roar that swells as Dave jogs around the bases, a roar that drowns out everything—the pretzel in hand, the cup of beer spilling over. It pulls me up, onto my feet, to join in the celebration.

As Henderson touches home plate, the dugout empties to shake his hand. The roar subsides, and people settle into their seats again, smiling at one another. We're in this together, one big happy family, at least to the bottom of the ninth. The sun warms us. A biplane circles overhead trailing a banner that reads, "You'll score at your Ford dealer." A hawk wheels through a cloudless sky. Steinbach, in the batter box, adjusts his cap and spits. The first-base coach lands a congratulatory pat on rookie Eric Fox's bottom. La Russa stands in the dugout, signaling to Ricky Henderson at second—two tweaks of the ear, a pat to the side of the head, a clap, arms to the side, thumb to the nose, three nods—yep, Ricky's gonna steal again. The euphoria continues. It envelopes the pimply college kid shouting, "Pee-nuts! Getchyer pee-nuts!"; the six-year old hopping up and down, twenty ounces of grape soda churning in his stomach; the old man with the A's visor and sunburned shoulders; the teenager in a shiny gold bikini top jiggling up the steps, and the entirely satisfactory sound of wood hitting leather.

Not a bad way to spend Easter Sunday, after all. ◉

> "According to American Health Magazine, a face-lift costs $3,500–$10,000; nose jobs are $2,000–$4,000; hair transplants are $5,000–$6,000 . . ."
> —Andrea Lo and Vera Perez

Compiled Report

To write a compiled report, you gather information about your subject from a variety of sources and present the results of your research in an informal summary. In the workplace this type of reporting is common in newsletters, brochures, and informal business reports.

Go to the Sources

Discussion: How do you make informed decisions? You go to the "sources" to find out what they have to say. And that's what we want you to do in this writing activity. Select a subject of interest (**a current event**, **an individual**, **a product**, **a procedure**, or **a career**) to investigate in three or more sources of information. Write a report based on the information you have compiled during your investigation. Provided below are basic guidelines to help you develop your writing. Also note the models following these guidelines.

Searching and Selecting

1. **Reviewing** • Review the headlines in the newspaper or a newsmagazine for writing ideas, or perhaps you could review a reference resource like the *Readers' Guide to Periodical Literature*. (Ask your librarian for other resources to review.)

2. **Searching** • Otherwise, consider subjects related to one or more of the general topic areas listed in the opening discussion. Is there an individual (or a group) you want to know more about? How about a product or a career?

Generating the Text

3. **Recording** • Gather information related to your subject from magazines, newspapers, pamphlets, etc. As you read each source, carefully note important facts, figures, quotations, and ideas. (Clearly identify the source of each quotation and statistic you record.)

4. **Reviewing** • Come to an informed decision or conclusion about your subject by reviewing all of the information you have compiled, and let that conclusion be the focus of your report. Then decide which facts and details best support your focus.

Writing and Revising

5. **Writing** • Write your first draft, working in details according to your planning and organizing. (*Note:* Before you actually get into the meat of your report, experiment with a few ideas for openings. See if you can come up with something that will really catch your readers' attention.)

6. **Revising** • Carefully review, revise, and refine your report before sharing it. Make sure each fact, figure, and quotation is accurate and that the source of the information is clearly cited. (Follow your teacher's guidelines for citing sources if they are provided. Otherwise, see how information is cited in the model reports or in your handbook. Provide a Works Cited [bibliography] page if your teacher requires it.)

Evaluating

? • • ? Is the report clearly focused around a timely, interesting subject?

Does the report include specific information from multiple sources?

Will readers appreciate the way the report presents information? Are sources cited properly?

Student Model

Student writer Michelle Wiersgalla compiled this basic report using two newspaper articles and a newscast as her sources. Note how the report moves smoothly from one source to the next, introducing new information and relating it to preceding ideas.

The opening lines answer *who?* *what?* and *when?* in relation to the subject.

The report summarizes information clearly and concisely.

In closing, the writer places this situation in historical perspective.

Russia and Moldova Face Imminent War!

API wire service reported on Tuesday, June 23, that Russian soldiers have joined the fighting in Moldova's civil war.

According to the *Racine Journal Times*, there has been long-standing ethnic conflict between Moldovans and Russians living in the area. Russian separatists have demanded autonomy and have declared an independent state. The *Journal Times* reported Russian soldiers from the region have joined civilians in fighting against Moldovans. Russian military officers deny giving orders to the soldiers and claim they joined their countrymen voluntarily.

An article in Tuesday's *Milwaukee Sentinel* reported Moldovan president Snegur has threatened war with Russia because of Russian military involvement. His may not be an idle threat: Moldovans recently attacked a Russian munitions warehouse, killing 26 soldiers. Moreover, the presence of Russian soldiers fighting alongside Russian civilians has increased the possibility of widespread violence within the former Soviet Union. Russian and Moldovan leaders met for peace talks Monday; however, prospects were said to be poor.

Russian president Yeltsin refuses to take steps to protect Russian residents in Moldova. In an interview Tuesday with reporter Peter Jennings, Yeltsin explained that he had hoped for a political, not a military, settlement. When Jennings pressed the issue, Yeltsin reluctantly admitted that the time for a political settlement had passed and that further violence would not be tolerated. Following the broadcast, political commentators speculated that this ultimatum could lead to more serious conflicts and possible war.

The legacy of the Russian people is one of violence, conflict, and political jockeying. The situation in Moldova promises to be one more page in a long and exhausting history. ◉

Student Model

The following model presents an interesting look at Charlotte Perkins Gilman, one of the early pioneers in the Women's Movement. Nichol Gilding, the writer of this report, gathered her information from four different sources: *American Women Writers*, *Contemporary Authors*, *Liberty's Women*, and *Who's Who in America*.

The opening paragraph presents background information.

This section summarizes a great deal of information clearly and concisely.

Chronological organization makes this report easy to follow.

Charlotte Perkins Gilman

Charlotte Anna Perkins was a writer and one of the early advocates of the Women's Movement at the turn of the century. She was born on July 3, 1860, and was raised by her mother in Hartford, Connecticut. Her father abandoned his family while Charlotte was a young woman, paying only for her schooling at the Rhode Island School of Design. His abandonment played an important role in forming Charlotte's beliefs of female equality and caused her to reject the commonly held notion of male superiority.

Such radical convictions did little to prepare the young poet and writer for a life of domesticity; yet, in 1884 she married Charles W. Stetson (*Liberty's Women*, 156). She gave birth to a daughter, Katherine, ten months later, and left shortly thereafter for California to recuperate from a pregnancy for which she was mentally and emotionally unprepared. It was here that Charlotte wrote a book about a pampered but emotionally strained woman who was locked in her room throughout her pregnancy. Unable to write or leave her room, she eventually suffered a complete mental collapse. In 1888, Charlotte and Katherine moved to Pasadena. This move was the beginning of Charlotte's more public and more vocal stance against sexism.

During the next four years, Charlotte used her writing skills to create feminist speeches, which she delivered to the increasing embarrassment of her husband Charles. In 1894 he filed for divorce, sparking scandalous gossip in California (*Liberty's Women*, 156). Following the divorce, Charlotte began editing the *Impress*, a major publication of the Women's Press Associate. During 1895-1900 she lectured on women's rights, and in 1896 she was sent to London as a delegate to the National Socialist and Labor Congress.

In June 1900, Charlotte married her cousin, George H. Gilman. The couple moved to New York and remained there for 22 years. Unlike her first husband, George Gilman supported his wife's beliefs. During their marriage, Charlotte became the sole editor of the *Forerunner*, a magazine of feminist views, articles, and fiction. Many of her own articles appeared in the magazine, which is still being published.

Charlotte Perkins Gilman contributed widely to the Women's Movement. She developed the idea of collective child care, attacked misconceived notions of womanhood and motherhood, and promoted the theory of female intellectual and political superiority.

As a writer, a lecturer, a speechmaker, an editor, and a political activist, Charlotte Perkins Gilman made a lasting difference in the Women's Movement. Women throughout the world owe her their gratitude. ◉

Student Model

The following report investigates the controversial topic of plastic surgery. Writers Andrea Lo and Vera Perez rely on their peers, medical professionals, and two magazines as resources for their work. (Reprinted from *Golden Gater Jr.* [June 28, 1991], which is published by the Center for Integration and Improvement of Journalism at San Francisco State University.)

Beginning with a candid quotation, the writers wait until the second paragraph to reveal the specific purpose of the report.

The report moves smoothly from one source to the next, blending facts and information into a unified whole.

High Price, High Risk = Beauty

"Yes, people should have plastic surgery if they want to, but God put what's on my face and I am satisfied with that so I'll keep it," said 18-year-old history major Christian Grayson.

With the number of cosmetic surgeries skyrocketing, the *Golden Gater Junior* took a closer look at this phenomenon . . .

Stella Blankenship, a registered nurse for the SFSU [San Francisco State University] Student Health Center, urged people not to whimsically jump into a serious surgery. Blankenship advised those considering reconstructive surgery to seek established doctors who can provide references.

Twenty-one-year-old English literature major Edna E. Rivera almost had a rhinoplasty (nose job), but changed her mind. "I realized my nose fit my face," she said.

Randy Fox, a psychology major who was formerly employed by a cosmetic surgeon, said, "I think it is baloney and most of it does not work. There are bad side effects; you should love yourself for who you are and what you were born with."

According to *American Health Magazine*, a face-lift costs $3,500-$10,000; nose jobs are $2,000-$4,000; hair transplants are $5,000-$6,000; and breast implants are $3,000.

American Health also reported that "most experts have discounted findings that rats with silicon implants develop cancer. Such studies, says the American Cancer Society, have little, if any, relevance to humans. Lab rats, they explained, grow tumors when implanted with almost any inert substance. The prevalence of breast cancer among women with implants is no greater than other women, say epidemiologists."

According to *Vogue* magazine, breast implants sometimes turn into "a hard, spherical appendage that looks abnormal . . . and is cold to touch and can sometimes be painful."

Vogue also said that liposuction is the most popular cosmetic surgery performed in America. To suck out the fat, *Vogue* reported, "a surgeon repeatedly thrusts a long, blunt instrument far into a patient's body, jarring loose the deep-seated fat." This procedure can lead to blood or fat clots that travel through the bloodstream and may lodge in the lungs or brain and lead to death. ◉

Professional Model

Brad Branan's compiled report about the privatization of the U.S. Postal Service relies on several key magazine articles and a book on business management. Notice how the writer uses quotations to integrate important material from his sources into his report. (This article originally appeared in the *Utne Reader*, Sept./Oct. 1995. Reprinted by permission of the author.)

Dead Letter Office?

Postal Service privatization: a return to the Pony Express?

The media relish bashing the U.S. Postal Service. Conservative pundits point to it as the classic example of the impossibility of providing good government service. And *Saturday Night Live* skits depict postal workers as either homicidal or so inept they could lose an elephant behind a cabinet.

Despite this poor image, the postal system remains vital to the goals and promise of American democracy. Its commitment to universal service means that any person can communicate with any other for the same low price (which is especially crucial since fax machines and e-mail are economically out of the reach of many Americans). And it provides a rare avenue of upward mobility for the thousands of minorities, veterans, and handicapped people it hires.

The harsh attacks that have been leveled at the system might explain why few have questioned the current restructuring of the Postal Service, even though it's likely to eliminate those democratic goals. In an effort to compete with e-mail, fax machines, and Federal Express, the Postal Service is turning over large parts of its work to the private sector.

This year, about 60 percent of the U.S. mail will be sorted by businesses, and there are plans to start contracting for postal delivery services as well, Sarah Ryan reports in the leftist economics magazine **Dollars and Sense** (Jan./Feb. 1995). Congressional Republicans want to sell off more of the Postal Service, and some suggest that the whole agency should be sold.

Critics cite a recent series of scandals in Chicago as evidence of how ill-prepared the Postal Service is for the information age. As reported by Jonathan Franzen in **The New Yorker** (Oct. 24, 1994), the problems were enough to make residents think twice before sending a postcard: Carriers left tons of months-old mail in their trucks, in their homes, underneath bridges. People lost phone and gas service because of bills that never came.

While an impressive 88 percent of Americans give the Postal Service high ratings in polls, the underlying problems that led to the Chicago mess can be found throughout the U.S. Postal Service, Franzen argues. "Although the postmaster general, Marvin Runyon, is fond of calling his $50-billion-a-year operation the eighth-largest corporation in the country, he labors under constraints that no private-sector CEO has to deal with," Franzen writes. That's because Runyon isn't a CEO—and those "constraints" are government regulations that keep the post office loyal to its democratic principles.

The writer hooks his readers with humor.

A statistic from one source establishes the current rate of privatization.

A story from another source illustrates the Postal Service problem.

In the tradition of the original Mayor Daley, the Chicago Postal Service has provided jobs for political reasons. Franzen suggests that political pork is bad business because many workers don't have the right skills or attitude for the job. "Maximal wealth and cutting-edge technology exist side by side with a second- or third-generation urban underclass for which employment at the post office may seem less a responsibility than an extension of its federally funded entitlements," he writes.

Likewise, Franzen sees the commitment to serving the urban poor —and by extension anyone who is poor—as a naive managerial principle. "With its mission of universal service, the Postal Service is like an urban emergency room contractually obligated to accept every sore throat, pregnancy, and demented parent that comes its way," he writes. That obligation stops the Postal Service from closing a branch office just because it's losing money. Franzen concludes that the Postal Service is a dinosaur that will never be able to compete with the new information technologies on its own.

But Runyon, the first postmaster to publicly support privatization, believes the agency that started delivering mail by horse can come of age. A former Nissan executive who stopped the United Auto Workers from organizing a plant in Tennessee, Runyon is restructuring the Postal Service to operate more like a business. He's currently asking Congress to give him greater leverage in contract negotiations with postal unions.

Runyon joins a growing group of leaders who think that business, free of the rigid demands of government bureaucracy, can provide services more efficiently. "While [privatization] does not exactly mean running government like a business, it does involve introducing corporate concepts to public service," Camille Colatosti writes in **The Progressive** (June 1993). Management guru Peter Drucker puts the matter a little more bluntly. "Government-owned enterprises stop performing as soon as political or social values interfere with the single-minded pursuit of profit," he writes in his book **The New Realities** (Harper & Row, 1989).

But if big business gains under this push of privatization, it's poor people who don't have fax machines, computers, or the money to use Federal Express who will probably lose. The private sector is lobbying Runyon and Congress to let them handle mail delivery as well as sorting, and there's widespread support among Republicans to end the Postal Service's monopoly on the delivery of first- and third-class mail. Ryan and Franzen both report that businesses are interested only in the profitable parts of the system. "As its most profitable parts are privatized [the Postal Service] will be forced to raise residential rates," Ryan concludes. It's easy to imagine low-income neighborhoods and low-density rural areas getting stuck with gutted, ineffective, and more expensive service. ◉

Support for the postmaster's position comes from two additional sources.

The writer concludes by stressing the ultimate "price" of privatization.

Academic Writing

"I don't want men accusing me of wanting to be a man if I choose a career. But I don't want women accusing me of surrendering to male dominance if I choose to be a homemaker."
—Melissa Meuzelaar

Essay of Definition

In an essay of definition, you clarify a complex term, idea, or concept by showing how the subject (1) fits within a particular class, and (2) is different from other members of its class. Defining topics in this way is common in argumentative essays, proposals, position papers, and technical reports.

"Words don't mean; people do."

Discussion: Write an extended definition of a commonly used term or concept that is not easily defined. It may be that the term is complicated (stock market, apartheid, cancer) or that it means different things to different people (love, courage, fairness). Select one (or more) of the following approaches in developing your definition: comparison/contrast, cause/effect, process analysis (how-to), negative definition (tell what it is not), explanation, or analogy. The following guidelines should help you develop your writing. For additional help, refer to "Defining Terms" in your handbook (546-547).

Searching and Selecting

1. **Selecting** • It's very important that you select a term or concept that is right for this assignment. Not just any term will work. It must be complex enough to require some real thought on your part; likewise, it should prompt your readers to think as well.

2. **Reviewing** • If no subject comes readily to mind, write freely about topics in the news, recent conversations, or personal reflections. (Or try thinking of terms people either misuse or use too freely, not carefully considering the real meaning of the terms.)

Generating the Text

3. **Collecting** • Write freely about your term, gathering details from dictionaries, interviews, song lyrics, personal anecdotes, films, newspapers, etc.

4. **Organizing** • Decide on your basic approach and how you want to arrange the details. You may want to begin with a dictionary definition and end with a negative definition or begin with a personal anecdote and end with how most people feel. Try a number of approaches.

Writing and Revising

5. **Writing** • There are several things to keep in mind when you start writing your definition. First, be sure to identify your term clearly and early. Second, help your readers understand why it's important to know more about this term. Also include enough comparisons, quotations, personal anecdotes, etc., to bring this term to life.

6. **Revising** • Review your first draft, thinking about what you've said and whether it offers your readers something new or different to think about. If not, look for a more creative approach.

Evaluating

Is the term to be defined an appropriate one?

Is the definition clear and supported in a variety of ways?

Are sufficient specific examples, anecdotes, and comparisons included?

Is the writing organized clearly and logically?

Student Model

Student writer Jason Borkenhagen defines sexual harassment using a variety of sources: a dictionary, interviews, newsmagazines, and a survey. The conclusion he comes to about sexual harassment is evident in the title: "It's Everywhere and Hard to Define." (This essay first appeared in the March 20, 1992, issue of *MHS Today*, a Milton [WI] High School student publication. It is reprinted with permission.)

The writer begins with a statement that gives the readers a clear overview of the article and a word-for-word dictionary definition.

Both students and teachers offer their feelings and experiences concerning sexual harassment.

The writer adds the results of a local survey and ends with a good news/bad news conclusion.

Sexual Harassment: It's Everywhere and Hard to Define

Sexual harassment is a problem many people in this country face today, whether in the workplace, school, or even at home.

The World Book Dictionary defines sexual harassment as "the harassment of a person because of her or his sex, as by making unwelcome sexual advances or otherwise engaging in sexist practices that cause the victim loss of income, mental anguish, and the like."

But sexual harassment is not a clear-cut crime. "Sexual harassment is such an undefined thing," math teacher Suzanne Shultz said. "It's not black or white like murder."

Oftentimes people accept sexual harassment as just part of the job or part of being female. Often they fear that if they complain, they will lose their jobs.

One junior girl explained her experiences with harassment: "At work there is a pervert that always puts his hands or arms around me, or says I have a nice body. He's been talked to two times about it. They should fire him!"

Throughout the month of October, sexual harassment cases seemed to jump out of the woodwork all across the nation.

This apparent outbreak came to light when Anita Hill accused Supreme Court nominee Clarence Thomas of sexually harassing her while they worked at the Equal Employment Opportunity Commission (EEOC), where Thomas was Hill's boss.

According to the Oct. 21, 1991, issue of *Newsweek*, reports of sexual harassment to the EEOC have increased from 3,661 reports in 1981 to 5,694 in 1990 (64 percent).

Harassment is not just a problem in the big businesses and cities. Right here in Milton we have our own cases of sexual harassment.

Sexual harassment is not just something people hear about anymore. In a survey of 140 students in grades 9-12, 30 have either been harassed sexually or know someone who has been. Of those who know someone who has been harassed, only 19 sought advice. Among teachers surveyed, 5 of 14 who responded said they had been harassed, but only one sought advice.

Nationally, 42 percent of women and 37 percent of men know someone who has been sexually harassed. Unfortunately, of those percentages, only 13 percent of the women and 11 percent of the men either have or know someone who has filed a complaint with the police. The good news is that these numbers are continuing to grow, which is just what it will take to bring sexual harassment under control. ◉

Student Model

The following essay uses interviews to explain and define "adultism." Notice how writers Lisa Yung and Tien Tuyen initially compare this term with other "isms" to establish it as a word that belittles or humiliates. (Reprinted from *YO! [Youth Outlook]*, the Journal of [San Francisco] Bay Area Teen Life [Winter 1991], published by the Center for Integration and Improvement of Journalism at San Francisco State University and Pacific News Service.)

In the opening paragraph, the writers invent a new term: "adultism."

The term's meaning is clarified through specific examples gathered from a number of teen interviews.

Prejudging is seen as another element of the definition.

ADULTISM: When Adults Humiliate Kids

Every adult knows about racism and sexism, but teens say another "ism" is just as humiliating. It's called "adultism." Teens experience it at home, in school, at the shopping mall, even in church—wherever adults fail to take young people's feelings seriously.

"It's like when your mom takes you shopping and leaves the dressing room curtain open," one teen explains. "How would she feel if someone did that to her?"

YO! interviews with teens identify some of the humiliating moments they've experienced as a result of adultism.

"Once I was driving with my uncle when our car ran out of gas right next to a stop sign that someone else had crashed into," recalls Tien Tuyen, 16, a student at Oakland Tech. "A policeman accused us of running over the sign. My uncle, who speaks no English, told me to talk to the policeman. But the officer told me to shut up because I was 'too young.' Afterwards, my uncle scolded me because he thought I had acted dumb."

Adultism is rooted in her family's culture, Tuyen believes.

"In the Chinese tradition, there are five basic relationships: ruler and subject, father and son, elder brother and younger brother, husband and wife, and friend and friend. In the first four, one person is always superior and another is inferior. (Only friends are equal.) The superior person assumes loving responsibility for the inferior and the inferior person shows respect and obedience to the superior."

Until she's 18, Tien is resigned to the fact that her family will treat her as an inferior. "My mom will complain about me all the time in front of my face. She'll expect me to obey her even when she humiliates me. When I object, she'll tell me that it's a life cycle, that when I'm old, I'll act the same way she does."

For Ayoka Medlock, adults who assume they know who and what you are, even when you say you're not, are guilty of adultism. "My mother sings in the choir at our church, so I usually watch my younger brother during the services," she says by way of example. "One Sunday a woman came up and started asking me all these questions about my brother. She assumed he was my child. When I told her he was just my brother, she didn't believe me. She walked away, saying, 'Yeah . . . sure!'"

Lisa Yung, 17, a senior at Pinole Valley High, says the main problem with adultism is that no one but teens knows it exists, and when you complain about it, people just laugh. But she experiences it regularly, especially when she walks into a business office or an expensive shop.

"Employees routinely ignore me until after they've waited on all the adults," she says. "Even in our school office, the receptionist told me she couldn't help me because she was on her lunch break. It was 10 a.m."

One teen argues that adultism is apparent only to its victims.

Yung believes adults treat teens like they barely exist because they assume all teens are rowdy, disrespectful, self-centered—much like one racial group stereotypes another. "The only way to stop adultism is for adults to treat teens with the respect each of us deserves."

Akilah Jeffery thinks one of the most potent forms of adultism is censorship. A 16-year-old junior at Skyline High, she recalls a particular episode with the school librarian. "I found this book called *Cannibal Nation: The Iranian People*. I wanted to check it out to see how racist it was, but she told me it didn't have a library card. 'Come back tomorrow morning,' she said, thinking I'd forget.

The writers add a powerful personal experience from another student.

"When I came back, the same librarian insisted she had no idea what I was talking about. When I looked for the book on the shelf, it was gone. Obviously, she thought I was too childish to be able to read the book without having it contaminate my mind."

When adults censor what we can read that way, they claim they're only acting in our best interest. They don't realize they're insulting our intelligence. In the end, it's we who have to educate them. ◉

Student Model

In the following essay, student writer Martina Lowry defines, explains, and clarifies the meaning of the word "tact." Note that she does an especially good job of summarizing the definition in her concluding paragraph.

The first paragraph ends with a basic definition of "tact."

A basic pattern of stating an element of tact, followed by an example, is set in the second paragraph.

The closing lines not only summarize the essay but also emphasize the importance of tact in society.

Break It to 'Em Gently

Many people in this world today need to be tactfully handled, and luckily there are people with tact. Tactlessness can hurt a person's feelings.   There is a boy in my gym class (I'll call him Bill) who has unbearably yellow, scummy teeth that gross everyone out.   Recently, another boy told Bill that he "should go Ajax" his teeth. Bill was crushed. Had the other boy been thinking, he would have realized that there is a better way to handle such a situation. He could have handled it with tact. Tact is the sensitive handling of situations that require conveying a potentially hurtful truth.

Sensitivity is a major component of tact. If a person isn't sensitive to another's feelings, there is no way he can be tactful. Children are especially vulnerable and must be handled sensitively. Sometimes a child's proudest accomplishments actually cause parents more work. Yesterday my 5-year-old brother proudly announced that he had cleaned the screen on our television set.   He was so proud of himself. Unfortunately, he used Pledge furniture polish which produced a smeared, oily film on the television screen. My mother smiled and thanked him for his efforts—and then showed him how to clean the screen properly. Her sensitivity enabled my brother to keep his self-respect. Yet, sensitivity alone does not make tact. It is possible for someone to be sensitive but not be tactful.

Truthfulness is another component of tact. A tactful person not only expresses herself sensitively, but truthfully as well. Doctors, for example, must be truthful. If her patient is paralyzed, a tactful doctor will tell the truth—but she will express it with sensitivity. She may try to give the patient hope by telling of new healing techniques under study or of advanced programs for handicapped people. A doctor would use tact with patients' relatives as well. Instead of bluntly saying, "Your husband is dead," a doctor would say, "I'm sorry . . ." or "He's no longer suffering pain." These are tactful ways of expressing the truth.

Tact should not be confused with trickery. Trickery occurs when a nurse is about to give a patient an injection and says, "This won't hurt a bit." Trickery occurs in the courtroom when a lawyer phrases his question so as to get the witness to say something he never meant to say. An admiring audience might say, "How tactful he is, this lawyer!" Clever he may be, but tactful he is not. The great difference between tact and trickery is truth. . . .

Sensitivity, truthfulness, and careful thought are all necessary components of tact. No one component will do; they must all be utilized in situations where people's feelings are at stake. Tact is a wonderful skill to have, and tactful people are usually admired and respected. Without tact our society would nurture insensitivity and disregard for others. ◉

Student Model

In the following student essay, Melissa Meuzelaar defines "feminism" in an attempt to classify herself. Compare this essay of definition to "Break It to 'Em Gently." How are these works similar? How are they different?

I Am *NOT* a Feminist

The writer argues that the dictionary definition is inadequate for describing "feminism" as it really exists.

The dictionary defines "feminism" as the movement to win political, social, and economic equality for women. However, the feminist movement doesn't stop where the dictionary definition stops. It defines itself according to the situation and the people involved.

Many feminists expect to be treated like men, dressing and acting like men, while others want the freedom to abort unborn children. Some feminists find pornography degrading, while others see it as an expression of art. Some feminists still appreciate chivalry, while others find it offensive.

I think that the feminist movement has stepped beyond the bounds of its definition and goals. Feminists have begun to ask for things that are not only impossible, but undesirable as well. They want to embrace the man's world as their own without regard for basic differences between men and women. They want the freedom to decide whether a child should live or die.

The writer offers specific examples to explain what she means by equality.

They want equality, and they think that equality means having the freedom to do whatever they want to do. They want equality, yet they often ignore the fact that equal does not mean identical. Radical feminists seem to begrudge men their sexual differences. They seem to think that true equality should negate the facts of life. They want men to have babies, too.

Equality means different but equal; it means sharing with men in the right to justice, the right to respect, and the right to make decisions. I want to be free to decide whether to be a homemaker or a career woman. I don't want men accusing me of wanting to be a man if I choose a career. But I don't want women accusing me of surrendering to male dominance if I choose to be a homemaker.

The writer emphasizes her individuality and her strong belief in being a person first, a woman second.

I want respect for the decisions that I make. I want respect for my vote on the school board. I want respect for how I raise and educate my children.

I want justice in court if I am raped. I don't want to be accused of seduction merely because I am female. I want the jury to look at the facts and make a just decision.

I don't want to be lumped into the feminist group and be treated like a man. I am a woman. I don't want to get a job because I am the token woman. I want to get a job because I am the best qualified.

I do share some feminist sentiments; however, I don't want to be labeled a "feminist." I AM NOT A FEMINIST; I am a woman who wants to continue to be a woman in a world where the capabilities and interests of the individual are what really matter. ◉

Professional Model

Writer Marilyn Frye clearly understands the necessity of defining abstract terms when discussing any important topic. In this excerpt, she presents her understanding and analysis of the term *oppression*. (From *The Politics of Reality*. Copyright © 1983 by Marilyn Frye. Published by the Crossing Press, Freedom, California.)

Oppression

It is a fundamental claim of feminism that women are oppressed. The word oppression is a strong word. It repels and attracts. It is dangerous and dangerously fashionable and endangered. It is much misused, and sometimes not innocently.

The statement that women are oppressed is frequently met with the claim that men are oppressed too. We hear that oppressing is oppressive to those who oppress as well as to those they oppress. Some men cite as evidence of their oppression their much-advertised inability to cry. It is tough, we are told, to be masculine. When the stresses and frustrations of being a man are cited as evidence that oppressors are oppressed by their oppressing, the word 'oppression' is being stretched to meaninglessness; it is treated as though its scope includes any and all human experience of limitation or suffering, no matter the cause, degree or consequence. Once such usage has been put over on us, then if ever we deny that any person or group is oppressed, we seem to imply that we think they never suffer and have no feelings. We are accused of insensitivity; even of bigotry. For women, such accusation is particularly intimidating, since sensitivity is one of the few virtues that has been assigned to us. If we are found insensitive, we may fear we have no redeeming traits at all and perhaps are not real women. Thus are we silenced before we begin: the name of our situation drained of meaning and our guilt mechanisms tripped.

But this is nonsense. Human beings can be miserable without being oppressed, and it is perfectly consistent to deny that a person or group is oppressed without denying that they have feelings or that they suffer.

We need to think clearly about oppression, and there is much that mitigates against this. I do not want to undertake to prove that women are oppressed (or that men are not), but I want to make clear what is being said when we say it. We need this word, this concept, and we need it to be sharp and sure.

The root of the word 'oppression' is the element 'press.' *The press of the crowd; pressed into military service; to press a pair of pants; printing press; press the button.* Presses are used to mold things or flatten them or reduce them in bulk, sometimes to reduce them by squeezing out the gasses or liquids in them. Something pressed is something caught between or among forces and barriers which are so related to each other that jointly they restrain, restrict or prevent the thing's motion or mobility. Mold. Immobilize. Reduce.

In this paragraph the writer goes to great lengths to explore a current claim made about oppression.

A need "to be sharp and sure" about oppression initiates a careful analysis of the term.

The difficult circumstances of being oppressed are explored in this section of the essay.

The mundane experience of the oppressed provides another clue. One of the most characteristic and ubiquitous features of the world as experienced by oppressed people is the double bind—situations in which options are reduced to a very few and all of them expose one to penalty, censure or deprivation. For example, it is often a requirement upon oppressed people that we smile and be cheerful. If we comply, we signal our docility and our acquiescence in our situation. We need not, then, be taken note of. We acquiesce in being made invisible, in our occupying no space. We participate in our own erasure. On the other hand anything but the sunniest countenance exposes us to being perceived as mean, bitter, angry or dangerous. This means, at the least, that we may be found "difficult" or unpleasant to work with, which is enough to cost one one's livelihood; at worst, being seen as mean, bitter, angry or dangerous has been known to result in rape, arrest, beating and murder. One can only choose to risk one's preferred form and rate of annihilation.

"Each family member then draws a slip. The one drawing the black dot is then stoned to death by the others. Everyone in the village including children and members of the victim's family participates in the murder."

—Todd Michaels

Literary Analysis

While writing an analysis of a literary work, you concentrate on your personal interpretation of the piece, using your initial thoughts and feelings about the work as a starting point or focus. You'll find literary analyses printed in newspapers and on book jackets.

Critically Acclaimed

Discussion: Write an analysis of a literary work (short story, poem, novel, or play). Your analysis should focus on your own insights and interpretations. (Do not refer to secondary [other] sources for additional ideas.) The scope of your analysis depends on the length and/or complexity of your subject. A short poem may be analyzed line by line, addressing a number of different elements; whereas the analysis of a novel or another longer work should focus on a specific aspect of the plot, setting, theme, characterization, or style. Refer to the models that follow and the guidelines below to help you develop your writing.

Searching and Selecting

1. **Searching** • Look for a poem, story, or novel that "speaks" to you, that has taught you something, that makes you smile or wonder. The choice is yours. (What about a work that confuses or puzzles you? Perfect. Your analysis could explore the cause or causes of your confusion.)

2. **Selecting** • If no subject comes to mind, ask your teacher or classmates for their recommendations. You might also ask your teacher if the assignment could be expanded to include nonfiction or other artistic works (movies, paintings, etc.).

Generating the Text

3. **Reviewing** • Make sure that you have a good understanding of your subject. Reread the text (or at least parts of it) if necessary, and review your class notes if the text was covered in class.

4. **Noting** • Think about different features of the text that you might write about. Are you drawn to a specific character? Would you like to analyze one of the themes or messages? Do you like how the writing sounds?

5. **Focusing** • State a possible focus for your analysis—a sentence or two expressing the main point you want to emphasize in your writing. Plan and organize your writing accordingly. (Make sure that you can support your focus with direct references from the source text.)

Writing and Revising

6. **Writing** • Develop a first draft, working in ideas and details according to your planning and organizing—or as ideas come freely to mind. (Make sure that the opening paragraph attracts your readers and identifies the focus of your analysis.)

7. **Revising** • Carefully review your first draft. Look for parts that are unclear, incomplete, or confusing. Revise and refine accordingly.

Evaluating

Does the writing present a thoughtful and thorough analysis of a literary work?

Is the purpose of the analysis clear?

Are the main ideas in the writing supported by direct references to the text?

Student Model

"The Lottery," a short story by Shirley Jackson, is a stark portrayal of evil set against a backdrop of everyday life in a small town. The following critical analysis by Todd Michaels focuses on the nature of that evil.

The Source of Horror in "The Lottery"

The writer opens by connecting the story to the reader's world.

"The Lottery" is a frightening story. Like any good scary story, it has monsters; but the monsters don't appear in the shape of vampires and werewolves. The monsters in "The Lottery" are the monsters that can be found in nice, average, decent people. People like you and me.

There isn't much action in the story. The people in a small village gather together on a beautiful summer day, men, women, and children. The children play and the grown-ups gossip or talk about their crops. With the arrival of Mr. Summers, ". . . who had time and energy to devote to civic activities," preparations for the lottery begin.

A basic summary of the plot reveals the evil nature of the lottery.

Names of families are placed in the "black box" and following an abbreviated version of what apparently was once a more complicated ritual, the heads of the families draw a slip from the box. The "winner" is the family representative who draws the slip with a black dot.

Blank slips of paper for each "winning" family member are put in the box. The slip with the black dot is used in place of one blank slip. Each family member then draws a slip. The one drawing the black dot is then stoned to death by the others. Everyone in the village including children and members of the victim's family participates in the murder. The lottery is concluded in time for the villagers to get home for lunch.

The full horror of the story comes through the juxtaposition of the revelation of the true nature of the lottery and the manner in which it is regarded by the participants and presented by the author. The narrative is presented flatly with no interior probing of the characters. Everything appears quite matter-of-fact and normal.

The lottery is seen as just another annual civic event like the Halloween program. The focus of the villagers' concern is on the details of the procedure to be followed, on questions like whether a new box should be made for the drawing. There is no real indication that anyone has any serious moral objections to stoning some village member to death.

A specific quotation from the text is incorporated in the analysis.

Someone does mention tentatively that other villages have stopped their lotteries, but Old Man Warner, the oldest surviving participant, scoffs at this notion, suggesting that soon "They'll be wanting to go back to living in caves." Given the nature of the lottery, Warner's defense of the lottery—that discontinuing it would be a step backward—is clearly ironic.

The original reason for the lottery is obscure. Warner's mention of "Lottery in June, corn be heavy soon" hints that it may have been some kind of sacrificial rite, but the real reason and indeed most of the ritual have been forgotten. What remains is the ritual murder repeated each year, tradition carried to its ugliest extreme.

At first the only emotion displayed by the villagers seems to be relief at not being the victim. Even the children of Mrs. Hutchinson, the woman to be stoned, smile when they discover they have not drawn the black dot. Worse, however, is the positive glee with which the villagers join in the stoning. It almost seems as if a blood lust is inherent in each villager. There is more here than just ignorance or an unquestioning acceptance of tradition. "The Lottery" calls into question the very nature of the human heart, and focuses our attention on the evil (or the monsters) lurking beneath the surface of civilized life. ◉

The final paragraph gets to the heart of the matter—that evil and blood lust are major forces in "The Lottery."

Student Model

In this model analysis, student writer Elizabeth Delaney explores the element of fear in William Golding's novel *Lord of the Flies*. Throughout this analysis, Ms. Delaney maintains her focus on the "beast" created by the boys on the island, exploring the implications of the beast's evolution in the text as well as in terms of our own human nature.

The first sentence states the thesis.

Throughout this analysis, specific examples are provided to support the writer's points.

Note the depth of the analysis in this paragraph. The writer carefully examines and tries to understand Jack's actions.

The Beast of Fear:
The Creation of a Beast in Lord of the Flies

In William Golding's novel *Lord of the Flies* the boys allow themselves to be terrorized by the beast because deep down they want it to exist. By creating a physical object to represent everything they are afraid of, the boys can base their fears on something tangible and distant, rather than something close and personal.

When they first arrive on the island, the boys have many tacit, implied fears: fear of being left on the island, fear of being on their own without adult assistance, fear of what may be occurring in the war from which they have fled, and perhaps even fear of not making a good show at being British. Consequently they all rapidly embrace the concept of the beast, for it is a way to externalize their fears. The British mind-set is characteristically one in which dwelling on personal trauma is a sign of weakness, and when coming to terms with pain, the reactionary British phrase is "never mind." What the boys want, therefore, is something they can fear in good conscience, some evil which does not stem from a past, present, or future in their own personal experience; so they place their discomfiture outside themselves and believe in a beast.

There are several clear-cut instances where precise, internal feelings become mixed up in the melting pot of fear which was the beast. The fear of not being rescued lessens as Jack's troupe of boys cease to be troubled by the prospect of remaining on the island since they are engaged in hunting the beast. The fear of not exemplifying standards for being British is wholly ignored when Simon is killed because he vaguely resembles the beast. The fear of what went on in their old world also leaves them, and even the littl'uns don't cry for their mothers as much as they cry over the beast.

Jack sums up the reason why externalized fear is so much easier to deal with than internal fear when he says, "If there was a snake we'd hunt it and kill it." It's a simple question of power. The boys never would have consciously thought that they were responsible for the incarnation of the beast, but they did believe they could be responsible for its demise. If the beast is something which can be destroyed, there is the potential for everything turning out suddenly all right, the possibility that all the evil which the boys perceive on their island could be purged with the removal of this one creature. In one sense Jack's cause is a noble one: purifying the world in which he resides of evil. However, he goes about looking for the beast in all the wrong places, and as a result, the boys commit several heinous crimes. In fact, part of Golding's message is that to "fancy thinking the Beast was something you could hunt and kill" is really catering to the true inner beast itself.

The development of the beast in *Lord of the Flies* is not an unusual one. As humans we are always looking for a beast, a scapegoat, something we can eradicate to solve all our problems. Mankind does not like to think that "what stands between him and happiness comes from inside him" (Golding, in an essay in reference to the novel). And, as the Nazis set out to exterminate the Jews, the Spanish Inquisition the heathens, and Stalin the freedom of the individual, so the boys, in a distinct, though minor, repetition of history, create the beast as a safety net, an outside evil to protect them from a knowledge of their true nature as fallen creatures, "beasts" themselves. ◉

In the final paragraph, the writer connects the beast in this book to the world at large.

Professional Model

This limited analysis by teacher and writer Ken Taylor explores Adrienne Rich's interpretations of loneliness as developed in the poem "Song."

"Song" by Adrienne Rich

The meaning and a great deal of the impact of Adrienne Rich's short poem, "Song," lies in the way the poet defines and interprets loneliness.

For most of us, "loneliness" carries a sad or an unhappy connotation. The word implies an unwanted isolation or separation from others and simultaneously implies a need for others. The *Webster's New World Dictionary* gives the second meaning for "lonely" as "unhappy at being alone." That is not how loneliness is presented in "Song."

In the first stanza of the poem, the narrator compares her "loneliness" to that of an airplane which ". . . rides lonely and level / on its radio beam, aiming / across the Rockies / for the blue-strung aisles / of an airfield on the ocean." The plane is alone, but it is going somewhere, toward the "blue-strung aisles / of an airfield on the ocean." Aiming for such a destination seems positive, and good, and almost magical. Loneliness in this stanza is anything but unhappy; instead, it is full of purpose and direction.

The second stanza, which describes a woman driving across country by herself, reinforces the idea of an individual who has chosen to be "lonely" for a purpose and indicates that real loneliness would be found in the "little towns she might have stopped / and lived and died in, lonely." In this line the narrator suggests that loneliness is not necessarily a condition of being physically separate from other people; she implies that any one of the small towns mentioned would have left her spiritually "lonely" because of their very sameness and drabness. She could have stopped at any one of them, but chooses not to. She seems much too full of purpose and control to give in to small-town loneliness.

The third stanza with its description of a person "waking first, of breathing / dawn's first cold breath on the city / of being the one awake / in a house wrapped in sleep" suggests a healthy sense of solitude and an equal sense of one's "differentness." Everyone else is sleeping. The narrator alone is awake to breathe "dawn's first cold breath on the city," awake and alive to the new day that the sleepers are missing.

The final stanza celebrates the poet's sense of her potential. She compares herself to an ice-bound rowboat on a wintry day, a boat ". . . that knows what it is, that knows it's neither / ice nor mud nor winter light / but wood, with a gift for burning." Like the rowboat, the speaker knows who she is. And like the rowboat's "gift for burning," the poet also has the "gift" to exert her individuality against those forces that would appear to shape or limit her. ◉

The writer focuses immediately on the key message in the poem.

A standard dictionary definition of loneliness establishes a starting point for the analysis.

The writer works through the poem stanza by stanza, discussing the different shades of loneliness as suggested by the poet.

Persuasive Writing

"Wife: Before I went to the Donna Reed School of Obedience, I was constantly running late. . . . Now, after taking courses in such subjects as ironing, cooking, vacuuming, and household fashion, my husband is happy as ever."

—Olivia Taylor

Ad Script

An ad script is a short "play" written for TV to promote an idea, sell a product, or make an announcement. When writing an ad script, you use sights, sounds, and words freely to achieve two goals: (1) grab the viewer's attention, and (2) hold it long enough to communicate the message.

"And now, a brief message . . ."

Discussion: We choose to watch shows on television for a variety of reasons. For years, we chose to watch the *Cosby Show* because the story of Dr. Huxtable and his family appealed to us: its characters were charming, the plots interesting, and the conflicts funny. We didn't, however, choose to watch the Jell-O, Levis, or Tidy Bowl ads that aired during the breaks, but NBC and its advertisers often tricked us into doing it anyway. Well, here's your chance to get back at these advertisers by learning a little something about the tricks they use. You will write your own television commercial script for a made-up product, remembering that the purpose of your script is to sell your product using the same tricks or techniques used by advertisers. Begin by studying ads on TV to see what kinds of images and ideas are developed. (These will be discussed in class.) Then refer to the guidelines below and the models that follow to help you develop your writing.

Searching and Selecting

1. **Searching** • Work with two other students to list 10 products you would like to sell: shoes, bungee cords, blue jeans, whatever.

2. **Selecting** • After each, list three possible names for your product and a description of who might buy it. Then select one product to sell.

Generating the Text

3. **Collecting** • Determine (1) what your product can do, (2) how it can do it better than related products, and (3) what kind of story (characters, plot, conflict) would best sell this product to your audience.

4. **Focusing** • Remember that you need to decide on one primary appeal, or hidden message, for your commercial, one that is right for the product and audience.

Writing and Revising

5. **Writing** • When you write the first draft of your ad, keep in mind you are writing for TV. Try to visualize what your ad will look like on the screen. Focus on telling a simple story, one with characters who have a fairly simple problem they are able to solve in 30 to 60 seconds. (Try to include camera and/or stage directions for your ad. Refer to the models for sample directions.)

6. **Refining** • Read your draft aloud and try "walking through" the actions with your group to see how the script sounds. Is it realistic and catchy enough to hold your viewers' interest? *Hint:* Studies show that if you can capture your viewers' attention for the first five seconds, they will usually watch the entire commercial.

Evaluating

Does the ad script tell a clear, clever story with characters, plot, and conflict?

Does the story make a strong enough appeal to convince a specific audience to buy the product?

Does the commercial utilize effective visual elements?

Analysis Sheet

Ad Script Analysis Sheet

Advertisers pay networks big bucks to broadcast their ad scripts. Why? Because the companies know that if they can hold your attention for the first five seconds of an ad, you'll probably watch the whole thing—**and** you'll buy what they tell you to buy. "NOT!" you say. "I think for myself, and I buy what I want." Really? You may believe that you buy what YOU want . . . but companies spend millions of dollars to convince you to buy what THEY want you to buy. Want to play like Michael Jordan? **Buy Nike shoes.** Want to look like a model? **Buy Cover Girl makeup.** Now neither company thinks that you'll really believe you're Michael or a famous cover girl; but both companies are willing to bet millions that you'll pay big bucks for the *illusion* of feeling lightning fast or looking superchic.

Watch an ad on the tube tonight—but be an active, critical observer. If you can, videotape it so you can watch it a half dozen times. Study the story. Analyze the sales pitch. You'll have to think about ads like those for Nike shoes or Cover Girl makeup because the messages are subtle. But other ads preach slogans—a word or phrase that's repeated so often you probably have it memorized:

You deserve a break today, so get up and get away, to . . . To what? What company cares about you enough to buy TV time so you'll take a break? The answer is **NONE.** Like all other advertisers, McDonald's restaurants want your cash, not your mental health.

To help you analyze the sales pitch, answer the questions below while you watch an ad. (The provided answers show how you might respond to an ad for a car.)

1. Product, service, message being advertised?
   Luxury sports car

2. Principal target audience?
   Upper-income males

3. Program airing commercial?
   NFL football game

4. Brief description of commercial's contents?
   A well-dressed businessman is shown driving his luxury car to work in the rain (summer), to an isolated mountaintop for a camping trip (autumn), to the city for an art exhibit (winter), and to the cliffs for a day of hang gliding (spring).

5. Slogan (or hidden meaning)?
   A man and a car for all seasons (Buy this car and you'll always be in style.)

6. Basic appeals used in commercial?
   Commercial appeals to status (car equals success). All-around type of guy, an individual, a Renaissance man. Rugged enough for camping, but appreciates art; macho, but sensitive; etc.

7. Argument of hidden message?
   This is the ideal man living the ideal life, and if you want to see yourself this way, go out and get this car. Then you can be an ideal man, too.

8. Additional reactions or observations?

Student Model

Student writer Olivia Taylor designed this satirical TV commercial to accompany the documentary television script she and her fellow students wrote, comparing the lives and presidencies of Eisenhower and Truman. The commercial satirizes the role of women in the 1950's, the general time frame covered in the documentary. (This script was developed by Ms. Taylor while attending the Center for Talent Development Summer Program at Northwestern University, Evanston, Illinois.)

The camera instructions are limited, providing only general guidelines and allowing the director flexibility in setting up the shots. This is standard practice for most television scripts.

Wife Obedience School—Fifties Style

CUT TO
Typical ANNOUNCER. Slicked-back hair and plaid-print suit jacket.

ANNOUNCER
You can't teach an old dog new tricks, but you can brush up on the old ones.

CUT TO
Lines of women ironing clothes. Wives practicing kissing husbands and then handing them briefcases.

ANNOUNCER (Voice-Over)
Send your wife to the Donna Reed School of Obedience. It will do wonders.

CUT TO
CLOSE-UP
Middle-aged wife superficially smiling at the camera. She is the stereotypical image of a fifties wife.

WIFE
Before I went to the Donna Reed School of Obedience, I was constantly running late. My husband was always complaining about everything I did. Now, after taking courses in such subjects as ironing, cooking, vacuuming, and household fashion, my husband is happy as ever. And so am I, because when he's happy, I'm happy.

INSERT PHOTOGRAPH
Typical fifties family. Similar to the Cleavers or Donna Reed's family.

ANNOUNCER (Voice-Over)
Make *Leave It to Beaver* a reality in your home.

FADE OUT

Reference is made to a popular family TV series of the '50s.

Student Model

Olivia Taylor also wrote the following satirical ad script for the documentary that compared the lives and presidencies of Eisenhower and Truman. The ad plays on the "Red Scare" theme that was so predominant in the '50s. (This script was developed by Ms. Taylor while attending the Center for Talent Development Summer Program at Northwestern University, Evanston, Illinois.)

The writer establishes the setting and describes the main characters in the opening camera instructions.

Board Game "The A-Game"—Fifties Style

INTERIOR DINING ROOM: EARLY EVENING
Stereotypical family of the times. FATHER—mid-thirties, wearing slacks, button-down dress shirt, and greased-back hair; MOTHER—mid-thirties, wearing collared dress and hair neatly pulled back; DAUGHTER—nine years old, wearing collared dress similar to mother's; SON—fifteen years old, wearing button-down shirt and jeans. All are seated around the dining-room table and a board game is set out in front of them. They are all engrossed in the game as the announcer is speaking.

ANNOUNCER (Voice-Over)
Tired of the constant threat of nuclear war? Have you always wanted the power to wipe out the communistic countries? Well now you can. With this new game, The A-Game, you can drop the atomic bomb on all the communistic countries that threaten your peaceful way of life. The rules are simple. Just move your tank around the board, picking up vital machinery to build your atomic bomb. Once you've completed your search, you simply answer questions on the reasons why communism is wrong. If you answer enough questions correctly, you go into sudden death where you match wits with the toughest commies. If you survive, you have won and get to push the button and . . .

Note how the announcer's description of the A-Game, the cuts to the family dining room, and the footage of the mushroom cloud work together to create the satire.

CUT TO

DAUGHTER cheering and pressing a red button in center of board.

ANNOUNCER (Voice-Over)
Look, Sis has just completed the final round and is dropping the atomic bomb!

INSERT FOOTAGE—KABOOM
Mushroom cloud appearing in night sky.

CUT TO

Dining room. Table and board game are burned. Family has been vaporized; all that is left is their shadows.

ANNOUNCER (Voice-Over)
Go out and get your game today. Just send in fifty cents and two box tops from Glow Bright Cereal. (Aside) This game may cause temporary loss of teeth and hair.

Professional Model

This 30-second TV ad script was created for a boat company running a spring tent sale. The video part (what you see on the screen) is described in italics. The audio part (called the voice-over—VO) is indicated in bold type. (This ad script is used with permission of Morse Advertising, Traverse City, Michigan.)

Note that a lot of territory is covered in this sales pitch: The purpose of the ad is identified, examples of new inventory are previewed, prices and package options are given, and a reason to buy is provided.

Spicer's Boat City Tent Sale

Opening Video and Graphics
The Big Boat Store is outside and under the big top . . . It's SPICER's big Spring Tent Sale.

Graphic: Tent Sale Bargains
With great Tent Sale bargains on everything at Spicer's . . .

Shot of model with graphic:
1992 2050 Capri, V6-MercCruiser Stern Drive (for co-op), full canvas, stereo, power steering, power trim and more
Like this big 20-foot Bayliner, a great big boat for the whole family—with V-6 MercCruiser Power and tons of extras, including trailer

Change Graphic:
$12,988 + freight and prep
Plus your choice of two free accessories packages!

List accessory packages:
O'Brien Ski Package-OR O'Brien Tube Package,
-OR-USCG Safety Package,
-OR-Eagle LCD Fish Finder
for under thirteen grand.

Quick shots of inventory (show pontoons)
Save on boats, motors, accessories, and hoists. Choose from cuddys and runabouts to pontoons and fishin' boats!

Exterior with Tent in Background; Add graphic
It's a great time to be outside and under the big top . . . at the Big Boat Store, Spicer's Boat City, your Mercury and Force Outboard Dealer!

:903 Close Sing
Spice up your life!

Professional Model

This television public-service announcement was developed for the World Wildlife Fund by Ogilvy & Mather Advertising. The announcement opens dramatically with a hunter pulling back a bow deep in the Amazon jungle. As the scene shifts from one impressive jungle scene to the next, words and phrases "pop on" silently (as shown on the script) and then fade. A final fade dramatically focuses on the word "Forever" until the end slide identifies World Wildlife Fund. The only audio is subdued classical music. (Reprinted by permission of Ogilvy & Mather Advertising and World Wildlife Fund.)

The words have been carefully selected for dramatic effect in this "silent" announcement.

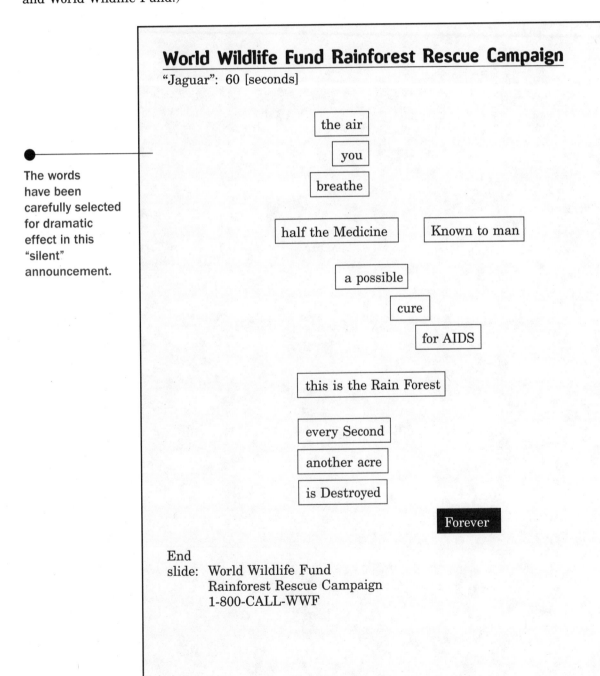

World Wildlife Fund Rainforest Rescue Campaign
"Jaguar": 60 [seconds]

the air

you

breathe

half the Medicine   Known to man

a possible

cure

for AIDS

this is the Rain Forest

every Second

another acre

is Destroyed

Forever

End
slide: World Wildlife Fund
Rainforest Rescue Campaign
1-800-CALL-WWF

"By printing so many articles on how to relate to guys, these magazines are giving teenage girls the impression that dating should be a major part of their lives. If it's not, there must be something wrong with them."

—Irma Johnson

Personal Commentary

When writing a personal commentary, you think about a subject and then present your own observations and ideas about it. Whether the tone of the piece is serious or playful, it is important to present clear, carefully thought out ideas. TV commentators and newspaper editors often write pieces of this type.

Up Front and Personal

Discussion: Write a brief personal commentary about some aspect of your immediate world or the world in general. Think of a commentary as one step removed from an editorial. An editorial expresses a specific opinion about a newsworthy event, often calling for a particular course of action or change to take place. A commentary makes a more evenhanded and reflective statement about life that may transcend or go beyond current events. It is more of a personal observation than a call to action. Nightly news broadcasts often include brief commentaries. Provided below are basic guidelines to help you develop your writing. Also note the model commentaries following these guidelines.

Searching and Selecting

1. **Reviewing** • Think about recent experiences or conversations for possible ideas. Also review your journal entries. A commentary could focus on some aspect of student life or on life in your community. It could focus on some aspect of the popular culture (MTV) or on something more essential to life (growing up).

2. **Brainstorming** • If you have trouble thinking of potential subjects, enlist the help of your classmates. A small group of you could brainstorm for ideas together.

Generating the Text

3. **Recording** • Write freely about your subject to see what you already know and feel about it and how much you need to find out.

4. **Assessing** • Review your initial writing and ask at least one classmate to react to your work as well. Continue collecting ideas and shaping your thinking.

5. **Focusing** • State a possible focus for your work—a sentence (or two) expressing the point you want your commentary to convey. Plan accordingly.

Writing and Revising

6. **Writing** • Write your first draft freely, working in observations and details that support the point or focus of your commentary.

7. **Refining** • Revise and refine your writing before sharing it with your readers. (Refer to the Proofreader's Guide in the handbook when you are ready to proofread your work.)

Evaluating

?·····? Does the commentary explore an issue that will be of interest to the intended readers?

Is a statement about this issue clearly (or cleverly) conveyed?

Is the writing sufficiently supported by details, examples, personal experiences . . . ?

Does the writing move clearly and smoothly from one idea to the next?

Student Model

In this short commentary, writer Mary Stephens discusses a phrase all too familiar to most young people—"grow up." The writer establishes one indisputable point in her work—adolescence is a challenging and often confusing time of life, pushing and pulling young people in a number of different directions.

An opening question immediately draws readers into the writing.

In the main part of the commentary, the writer discusses what "growing up" means.

Grow Up!

"Don't you think it's about time you grew up?" If you're like me, you've probably heard this—or something like it—many, many times. Although most people pretty well understand what is meant by "growing up," not everyone knows just how you're supposed to go about doing it. Part of the problem is that no two people ever grow up in the same way, at the same time, with the same results. For most young people, growing up means being told to act like an adult, while being treated like a child. It means having an abundance of advice but a shortage of patience. It also means wanting to be independent, but realizing just how dependent you still are. Growing up means having many possible directions to go in and not knowing just which one will work best for you. It means slowly being recognized as an individual, with personal hopes, dreams, and desires, rather than as someone's son or daughter. It means finally letting go of the bar and flying, not knowing if a net is beneath you. And, above all, growing up means making many mistakes, but learning along the way. Luckily, no one expects you to grow up all at once—or all alone. About the only thing we know for sure is that growing up requires no previous experience—just an active mind, patience, and faith in your own abilities. ◉

Student Model

In this commentary, Irma Johnson focuses her attention on magazines aimed at young teenage girls. Because these magazines focus almost exclusively on boys—what they think, what they want, how to get one—the writer feels young readers are getting a warped perception of what it means to be a teenage girl. (This article first appeared in *New Youth Connections: The Magazine Written By and For New York Youth*, November 1991.)

Like most good commentaries, this one stems from the personal experiences of the commentator.

The writer makes the point that magazines *create* as much as *reflect* the thinking of their readers.

The writer cites many examples to illustrate her point.

Wanna Life? Get a Boyfriend!

I used to be an avid reader of teen magazines. From when I was 10 until I was 13, I devoured *Seventeen* and *YM* every month. I was just becoming a teenager and I wanted to know how I was supposed to act and what I was supposed to do. The magazines had everything I was interested in (or thought I was interested in)—information on clothes, makeup, and boys.

The magazines told me that to be normal and happy I had to look good and have a boyfriend. But I wasn't as pretty or as thin as the models. I wasn't dating yet either. Every time I read another article on how to deal with your boyfriend, I would feel as if there were something wrong with me. The feeling that I didn't quite measure up stayed with me for years.

Eventually, I matured and realized that I was perfectly normal and that the magazines were giving me a wrong message. Looking back, I'm glad that I didn't start dating then. I realize now that if I was so easily influenced by some dumb magazines, I probably wasn't ready.

BOYS, BOYS, BOYS

Teen magazines haven't changed since then. The August issue of *YM* had an article on how to get guys to commit; an article on guys' biggest dating disasters; and two girls' opinions on whether they would date a guy that their best friend had a crush on.

In the August issue of *Seventeen* there was a fashion spread on sweaters featuring a girl who is distressed because her boyfriend is going away to college. In the August *Sassy*, I found an article called "Chronic Long Distance Boyfriend Distress." What I didn't find was even one article on girls who don't have boyfriends and don't want them.

As if that weren't enough, two of these magazines devoted entire issues to guys. *Seventeen's* July "Boy Crazed" issue had more than 10 articles and photo spreads about guys. There was a quiz to help you rate your boyfriend, a photo spread that followed two boy-crazy girls on their hunt for Mr. Right, and an article about the winners of *Seventeen's* "Best Boyfriend Contest" featuring quotes from their lucky girlfriends and pictures of the happy couples.

YM's April "Major Guy Issue" had about the same number of articles and photo spreads on the subject, including "How to Survive the First 60 Days of a Relationship" and a quiz to help you figure out whether your relationship is healthy or harmful.

JUST FOR FUN

By printing so many articles on how to relate to guys, these magazines are giving teenage girls the impression that dating should be a major part of their lives. If it's not, there must be something wrong with them.

Where are the articles on resisting peer pressure to date or how to have a successful friendship? Not in *Seventeen* or *YM*!

Instead, these magazines give us articles like "100 Guys Talk—What 100 Guys Had to Say about Love, Sex, Dating and You" (April *YM*); "Real Back to School Clothes . . . Rated by Real Guys" (August *YM*); "Why Guys Love Long Hair" (July *Seventeen*); and monthly columns like "Guy Talk" in *Seventeen* and "What He Said" in *Sassy*. In short, guys' opinions on everything—especially clothes and dating.

Articles like these tell us that what guys want is very important and that we should keep their likes and dislikes in mind when we decide what clothes to buy, how to wear our hair, and how to act. Girls' opinions, on the other hand, are limited to letters and reader polls. Why don't they have girls rate outfits?

. . . A magazine can inflict an enormous amount of pressure on teenage girls—especially younger teens who don't really know what they want. Younger girls view teen magazines as handbooks on how to be a teenager. I know I did. Teen magazines can influence how girls act as much as they influence how girls should look. They shouldn't, but they do. ◉

Note all of the specific facts and details presented in this commentary.

The writer's main point about teen magazines is clearly expressed in the closing.

Student Model

An object we seldom think about—the eraser—is the subject of Kristi Wilt's entertaining commentary. This model has the same flavor as the personal commentaries that conclude *60 Minutes*, the popular television news show.

A clever opening naturally draws readers into the commentary.

The writer relates a personal experience about her subject.

Erasers' unusual uses appear in a modified list.

The play on words in the closing reinforces the playful tone maintained throughout the writing.

The Point of an Eraser

Without some modern appliances we have today, life would be a whole lot tougher. Without dishwashers, we would have dishpan hands; without showers, we would be dirty; without deodorants, we would be smelly; and without one of the greatest discoveries of all time, something that makes us flawless, we would have to admit we make mistakes.

This near-perfect device is the everyday, special, one-of-a-kind, small pink eraser. They come on tops of pencils and pens, and even by themselves. Without them, man would be frustrated, stressed out, and left with messy papers.

As kids, we all look forward to the first day of school. School means friends, fun, and the famous school supplies. As a child, I loved a new, never-before-sharpened pencil most. As I gaped at the perfect structure of this writing utensil, I imagined the point it would soon have.

My eyes traveled over the six-sided object to the shiny silver end, and then to the top—the eraser. I always loved to have it but hated to use it. Using it would mean breaking it down. I would be left with messy scratch-outs all over my papers. Teachers would be annoyed, parents upset, and bosses mad. Just thinking about it gave me shivers.

Erasers also have many uses that we don't give them credit for:

(1) Girls and, nowadays, even guys know what it's like to lose the back of an earring. Without the back the front can't stay on. What to do? Get a piece of an eraser and stick it on. They work wonderfully.

(2) Doorstoppers. Yes, doorstoppers. The rubber eraser will stop any door from closing—for 49 cents!

(3) How many times have you put a pencil behind your ear only to have it fall out the other side? Obviously, the pencil you're using is eraserless. Don't ask me how, but erasers help stick the pencil to your head. Maybe that shiny silver thing at the end is slippery or something.

And last but not least, (4) when was the last time you were annoyed at someone for tapping an eraserless pencil on a desk? With an eraser, the tapper can tap without getting on your nerves.

Well, there you have it; one of the modern appliances of today we couldn't do without.

Because, if we didn't have erasers, . . . well, let's just erase the thought from our minds. ◉

Professional Model

In this commentary, Eugene Kane of the *Milwaukee Journal* takes issue with the cliches found in popular song lyrics. He does so by giving a few examples of the lyrics he finds irritating, and then explaining exactly what's wrong with them. Kane's tongue-in-cheek suggestions for improving popular song lyrics add humor to his commentary. (This article first appeared in the June 30, 1992, issue of the *Milwaukee Journal*. Reprinted with permission of the *Milwaukee Journal*.)

Lyric Critic Offers Tips from Heart

The author introduces his subject with a personal reflection—it's clear from the beginning what he's talking about and how he feels about his subject.

As somebody once said, you'd think the world would have had enough of silly love songs by now.

Most of the songs I hear on the radio are love songs. That doesn't seem right; there's got to be at least one other subject worth writing about. But my biggest complaint is that the lyrics to all of these love songs are so similar, it's like listening to that same love song over and over.

Take this popular refrain: "I love you, girl, you're the finest girl in the whole wide world."

There are at least 15 songs with that hook. Evidently, music lyrics are still one of the few places where you can call a woman a "girl" and get away with it. The feminist movement must have given songwriters special dispensation because it's so hard to rhyme anything with such adult references as "woman," "lady," or "female."

Here's another one of my favorites: "You're the one that I love, you're like an angel sent down from above."

Love, Angel, Above?

Kane divides his commentary into three parts: introduction, critique, and suggestions for improvement.

If I hear that corny line one more time, somebody's gonna get their wings ripped off. Once again, we have evidence of a rhyming quandary. If you write a love song with a lyric that ends with the word "love," it must be mandatory to match it with another line that ends in "above." I suppose the only logical continuation of that theme is to have an angel coming down from above to complete the image. Of course, the angel is supposed to be analogous to the loved one for whom the song has been composed. That's easy enough to follow, right?

But my gripe is that (1) the angel coming down from heaven reference is a bit too heavy in the religious imagery department for my taste, and (2) most people who have ever been in love already know the experience is a lot closer to that other place than it is to heaven.

"You mean the world to me . . . I would place no one above you."

A lot of love songs have this catchy refrain, no doubt a way of assuring a loved one that he or she will always come first. But, again, my problem is that it makes no sense. Sure, you might not place another person above your loved one, but what about a thing, or a place? For example, a lot of men are guilty of placing sports ahead of their loved ones, and some women would rather watch a favorite soap opera than spend quality time with a lover or spouse. So once again, the line is tired, and it doesn't really say much. And, this line is merely a reworked version of the "love" and "above" quandary discussed in earlier paragraphs.

Some Suggestions

Let me propose here a few suggestions, some fresh combinations that will free songwriters from having to resort to the same tired cliches in their lyrics.

How about something like "I love you like a fool, you make my mind feel like a whirlpool"? Here, we are able to create an enchanting new love-phrase, "love you like a fool" instead of the tired "I'm losing my mind" and rhyme it with the equally innovative "whirlpool" analogy. Which, after all, is what love is actually like, anyway.

Or: "You are the only one I love, you make me feel like giving you a shove." Here, we eliminate the usual "love" and "above" rhyme, replacing it with "shove," which instead brings forth a new dynamic, ergo, that love is a double-edged sword and we sometimes have unspoken animosity toward our loved ones that can turn violent.

"You mean the world to me, I'll never let you leave, so sue me."

Again, a topical reference that speaks to the constant litigation that surrounds the marital contract.

There are plenty more where these came from, songwriters. All you have to do is use your imagination a little bit. Or start dating the same women I date. ◉

Side notes:

In his critique, the writer presents different love-song lyrics and analyzes them.

A playful tone is maintained throughout the commentary.

Professional Model

In this personal commentary, Hannah Hinchman expresses her feeling that the wilderness ought to be regarded as a home and sanctuary for the animals that live in it, just as her cabin is her own sanctuary. Note the way Hinchman frames her commentary by beginning and ending with images of her home. (This commentary first appeared in *Sierra* magazine in the spring of 1992. It is reprinted by permission of the author.)

Home Free

Note how the "heavily trodden" trail differs from the "wild country" through which the writer tracks an elk.

Hinchman makes her point by reflecting upon her firsthand observations.

Tonight, curled up on the couch while snow fills the fir branches outside, I sketch the interior of my cabin. It is a small domestic tableau: the pale light on a table top, the candle in the window, the shadows under the eaves. I look around, pleased at the warm glow of lamps and the tick of the fire. Later the cabin may close in and all these corners seem stale and cramped, but at the moment everything fits like a ground squirrel's burrow.

Earlier today, before the new snow began to fall, I set out into the Teton Wilderness. The trail was heavily trodden by horses and hunters, churned to slush and refrozen into ruts that forced me to keep my eyes on the ground. Elk and moose trails crossed at right angles, the animal's flight from the hunters evident in the long strides, splayed toe marks, and scattered snow.

As I traced the steps of an unhurried elk the sense of being in wild country returned, affirmed by tracks of many animals going about their business undisturbed. The tracks led to a clearing and an elk's bed, which I sat down in. Here was wildness as we talk of it; but sitting in the elk's body shape, seeing what it had seen as it stopped here, made me think of my cabin and its familiar interior. I can't say whether the elk is pleased by the look of the clearing, but it knows this place, it knows it is at home.

I walked further, then stopped again where bounding mouse tracks led to a snow tunnel that descended to a fallen log. The passage, lit by a serene, diffuse blue light, opened out on an interior courtyard of moss and spruce needles, then disappeared into darkened wood-and-earth corridors. Deep quiet, no drafts, a stable temperature, body-shaped rooms: A mouse would return to this spot with relief.

The multitude of tracks revealed an abundance of dwellings; almost every log, bank, and thicket, it seemed, had been selected and renovated. When the tracks disappeared into a snow tunnel with a generous, polished, south-facing terrace, I wanted to enter too, stroll the corridors, settle down on a pile of shredded grass, and sketch the shadows beneath the eaves.

To be home. It's an ordinary, unexamined condition for us, set against the wildness we head out to find. This time, though, the wild hills seemed full of a devoted domesticity, of well-appointed rooms and comfortable beds.

The trail I followed back to my own home was easy to walk on: A hunter had dragged the heavy body of an elk along it, and the snow was flattened and streaked with fresh red blood. Approaching my cabin, in a little gathering of similar structures, I felt the way I sometimes do in the wilderness: This human domesticity seemed unknowable, unpredictable, a source of danger. It was several hours before I was again able to see my cabin as a snug, welcoming burrow. To the animals whose homes border our fences, the settlement is the wild place. ◉

"One might argue that plenty of useful shows exist, but how many kids out there actually spend their average three to five hours a day watching programming they'll remember a year later?" —Camberley Crick

Essay of Argumentation

In an essay of argumentation, you try to convince your reader that your position on an issue is correct. To do this, you need strong, clear arguments to support your own view and to show the weaknesses of opposing views. Such writing is common in research papers, business proposals, and application or sales letters.

"Now this is the way I see it . . ."

Discussion: First, choose a topic about which it's possible to write the following: (a) a proposition or statement that you will argue for, (b) argument(s) supporting your proposition, (c) argument(s) opposing your proposition. Second, look for information (evidence) with which to build arguments for and against your proposition. And third, use the information to write an essay that convinces your readers that your proposition is right. The steps below outline the process. For more help, see "Thinking, Logically" in the index of your handbook, and read the model essays that follow.

Searching and Selecting

1. **Searching** • In groups of three or four, list 10 questions or problems you hear debated locally or nationally. (Don't choose silly ones like whether crew cuts look weird, or overused ones like abortion rights.)

2. **Selecting** • Together, choose one of your topics and put it to the test by trying to address it in the following ways: (a) a logical proposition (central claim), (b) an argument supporting the proposition, and (c) an argument opposing the proposition.

Generating the Text

3. **Collecting** • Look in books, magazines, or newspapers for information. Take notes, especially on strong arguments supported by the opinions of authorities and by factual evidence. Label arguments "pro" (for your proposition) or "con" (against).

4. **Assessing** • Check the best pro and con arguments. If you need to change your central claim in order to better defend it, do that now.

Writing and Revising

5. **Writing** • Consider what you will say first, second, . . . last, and go to it. If you're stuck, ask a classmate to be your ear: read the proposition and talk through the argument. Ask your partner to restate the proposition and discuss which arguments sound most or least convincing. Adapt and write. (*Hint:* Save your best pro argument as the final knockout punch.)

6. **Revising** • Review, revise, and refine your argument before presenting it to your readers. Have a classmate review your writing as well.

Evaluating

Is the proposition reasonable and clearly stated?

Are supporting arguments logical, clear, and convincing? Are opposing arguments dealt with?

Given the supporting arguments, is the conclusion valid?

Student Model

Student writer Eric Van Ruler addresses his argument in the form of a letter. Because this argument involves emotions as well as facts, the letter creates the necessary distance between both sides. Note how the writer carefully addresses issues he knows concern his parents.

The writer states his proposition and explains the letter's purpose.

Throughout the letter, the writer shows respect for the other side of this argument.

Dear Mother and Father,

I am writing you this letter on the issue of my getting a motorcycle. I decided to do this since every time we try to talk about it we end up in a disorganized yelling match and get nothing accomplished.

I realize that you are worried about my safety, but there are dangers in nearly all things including driving cars and playing sports. Many people are hurt every year in car accidents and sporting events, but just because there are dangers involved in these activities does not mean we should avoid them. Motorcycles are not that dangerous if they are ridden responsibly and the driver is alert and cautious. You say that what frightens you is that most times in accidents in which motorcycles are involved, it is not the rider of the cycle, but the driver of the car, who is at fault. This is normally because the driver simply didn't see the cyclist. This is true, but you let (or shall I say made) me drive that moped for over a year. You must agree that it is easier to see a motorcycle than a moped.

I would now like to address the point that Dad brought up. Yes, I must agree motorcycles do have a lot of power or even as you said "excessive power." I also cannot argue with the fact that the tendency of almost all teenaged guys, me being no exception, is to now and then use that power. I hope that you will trust me in this area since there is no way for me to prove myself until I have a motorcycle. I believe that at this point I am mature enough to handle this responsibility. Please give me the chance to prove it.

Finances will not be a problem. I have enough money in my account to buy the Night Hawk and to pay for insurance, but if you think that I will be cutting it too close, I will consider buying the Kawisaki LTD. We will talk about this after you have read this letter and considered what I have said.

Naturally I hope that after you have read this letter, you will see things my way; but if you don't, I will do my best to discuss it rationally and I hope you will too.

Truly,
Eric Van Ruler

Student Model

Student writer Camberley Crick uses personal experience as a springboard for her arguments in favor of reducing the amount of television viewing in the lives of students. Her essay includes comments on both the negative effects of too much TV and the positive benefits derived from reducing television-viewing time. (Reprinted from the June 1992 commemorative issue of *High School Writer* with permission.)

Unregulated TV Viewing Is Bad for Kids

The opening paragraphs describe the circumstances leading to the author's reduced television viewing.

Four years ago my father pulled the plug on the Crick family life-support system, our television. For months he had tried different ways to keep us away from the little black box; but whenever his back was turned, my brothers, sister, and I would tiptoe downstairs and bathe ourselves in the TV's glow. After a while my father wised up and attached a small gray box to the wall. Behind its locked door hid a timer, allowing him to supply the power to the TV for a given amount of time. We were not to be stopped by this, though. After realizing we couldn't pick the lock on the box, a new way around the mountain was discovered. Using an extension cord, we were able to plug the TV into the bathroom wall socket. Unfortunately, this plan of attack was discovered after a few short weeks. My father told the cable company to disconnect us, and since then we have been deprived of television.

Recently some crude contraptions resembling TV antennas constructed out of coat hangers have been found connected to the television, but in general, all the kids have adjusted to living without. Because I have had firsthand experience with the benefits and drawbacks of living without the tube, I can offer insight into this matter.

Benefits of "living without TV" are listed.

The benefits of living without TV include having more time, better grades, being less influenced by commercials, and avoiding the depths of "couch potatoism."

Most television today is junk. It has a special way of holding the viewer hostage for hour after hour, no matter how dull the show. An unsuspecting kid will sit in front of the screen with the intention of watching just one show, and then stay for four or five. One might argue that plenty of useful shows exist, but how many kids out there actually spend their average three to five hours a day watching programming they'll remember a year later?

The writer discusses the negative effects of overexposure to television.

When TV was available to my family, school never claimed much of my time or interest. Grades have improved dramatically for all members of my family now. Statistics show that the number of hours spent gazing inertly at the television are inversely proportional to grades received at school.

Watching television is a reactive occupation. It takes absolutely no skill or thinking. Some people complain that video games, like Nintendo, are equally bad for kids; but at least they take some sort of movement and coordination. Television allows us to sit without motion for hours while our brains turn to mush. If parents don't shut off television, or at least regulate its watching, the "Homo lackadaisicus" (more commonly known as the couch potato) will take over. ◉

Student Model

Student writer Jennifer Nanna's essay is a response to the U.S. government's decision to intervene in the Persian Gulf Crisis in 1990. She presents a well-organized argument from start to finish. (This model first appeared in *Moments* [1991], a collection of student writing from Badger High School in Lake Geneva, Wisconsin.) *Note:* This essay was written before Desert Storm.

The writer uses the opening paragraph to share some recent history, closing with her proposition.

Arguments opposing the proposition are addressed early.

The author's strongest pro argument (the killing) is introduced here.

The pro arguments continue in this section.

Price of War

Throughout history, disease, poverty, crime, and war have plagued Americans. For the most part, these ills of society are difficult to control. Regardless of the precautions Americans take to rid themselves of these misfortunes, they affect (excluding war) every town in every part of America. One of the more serious conflicts that Americans have faced is war. Recently, for example, when Iraq invaded Kuwait on August 2, 1990, the United States was faced with the choice to ignore it or intervene. On August 3, the United States chose to intervene in the Persian Gulf Crisis. However, it is in the United States' best interest to take a defensive position and avoid an all-out war with Iraq.

Although America's reputation would be enhanced as a world power if the United States won the war against Iraq, it is not certain by any means that this would actually happen. Iraq has one of the largest armies in the world, numbering over one million soldiers. This compares with the 400,000 U.S. servicemen in the gulf.

While it may seem that the Iraqi soldiers are tired after fighting Iran for nine years, the truth is that this lengthy war hardened many boys into seasoned soldiers. Also, the Arab nations view death differently than Americans. Americans perceive death with fear and apprehension, whereas the Arabs would go to any length to fight for what they believe. For the Iraqis, death is more of an obstacle than a final outcome. They won't hesitate to kill. This is a paramount point to remember, considering Iraq is expected to develop the technology for the nuclear bomb in eight to nine months.

Many Americans think the price of oil will continue to escalate if Americans don't go to war to settle this crisis. This, however, is a narrow viewpoint that is unlikely to happen. As soon as the first shot is fired in the gulf, Hussein has threatened to push a button that will blow up the oil rigs in Kuwait. This catastrophe will lead to an expensive and lengthy operation to rebuild the oil wells.

Furthermore, if we fail at war, our reputation as one of the top three world powers may deteriorate. In the eyes of the other two world powers, China and Russia, and others, we may appear "soft." As Americans it is our duty to realize that we cannot successfully be world policemen, which is evident by our past mistakes. In 1950, we felt the need to come to South Korea's rescue, and, as a result, the United States and South Korea lost 580,000 men. In 1958, again it seemed our responsibility to come to South Vietnam's aid, and we came out of the war without victory and with 55,000 deaths. In both wars, the question was asked: Why are we here? If we go to war with Iraq, many Americans will be angry at the lack of direction from President Bush and become indifferent towards the war.

In addition to this, we as Americans must think about the financial state of our country. After the rapid growth in the 1980's, our economy has slumped into a recession that has forced Americans to be more frugal. Meanwhile, millions of dollars are being sent to our soldiers in the Middle East. Already, Operation Desert Shield has cost 17.5 million dollars. While our allies profess their utmost support in stopping madman Hussein, it is the United States that is paying for 90 percent of the effort. This drainage of resources is increasing our high national debt.

And most important of all, many innocent men and women will go to war fighting for a cause they can't understand, striving to put their finger on why they are over there. If the United States engages in war, devoted men will be brutally killed over something that could have been resolved through negotiation. This is the real tragedy of war— the loss of each and every life.

Thus, it is up to the United States to take a defensive position and avoid an all-out war with Iraq in the upcoming months. Our nation cannot afford to fall as one of the top three world powers. Our nation cannot afford the extreme cost of such an event. And finally, our nation cannot afford to lose thousands of men and women to war, where even they can not see the reason. The trauma and holocaust of a war with Iraq would make the problems of society, such as disease, poverty, and crime, pale in comparison. ◉

The loss of life is again presented as the author's strongest argument against all-out war with Iraq.

The author clearly restates her proposition, along with her three strongest pro arguments.

Professional Model

Ken Taylor, an English teacher and writer in New York, proposes that students be given "professional student" status. He argues that paying students to achieve in high school will directly affect those most in need of an incentive . . . and in terms they are likely to understand and appreciate.

The opening paragraph presents the problem to be addressed.

A proposal is presented to make "academic rewards" more equitable.

In support of his plan, the writer offers a main reason for students dropping out.

The final paragraph restates the "payment proposal" as one that could work.

Learn to Earn

Whenever the subject of America's educational ills arises, which is fairly frequently of late, the lack of student motivation is always a prime target for discussion. How, people ask, can we motivate our students to learn? How can we, in fact, keep them in school long enough to learn? (In some urban areas the drop-out rate has reached astronomical proportions, particularly among non-native English-speaking students and certain other groups.) The answer to this problem is, I feel, quite simple. Give them money. Pay students to go to school.

It's not as though we aren't already engaged in bribing students to attend school. The whole thrust of academic and other types of scholarships is based on monetary rewards for being a good student. Calling a cash award a "scholarship" doesn't alter the fact that what's being offered is still money. So, what about the student that doesn't want to go to college? Where is that student's reward? Why should only the "best students" or the "best athletes" pick up all the cash? Why not let all the students in on the act? Why not pay everyone for going to school the same way they would get paid for doing any other job?

In some states the parents of students are being denied part of their public assistance payments if their children do not attend school on a regular basis. So what we are saying to these people is, if you don't go to school, the state will shut off part of your parents' income. Well, why not turn it around and send a positive message? Why not say to those students, if you go to school, you can make more money?

In many urban schools one of the main reasons students drop out of school is because they are forced by family circumstances to work what amounts to a full-time job while they are attending school. When it comes to a choice between going to school or going to work, going to work usually wins out for very practical reasons. If these same students were paid a minimum wage for attending school, they wouldn't have to worry about choosing between education and keeping their jobs. In the long run, it would probably be less expensive to keep these students in school by paying them than to have them drop out of school with no real job skills, ultimately ending up on some kind of welfare assistance.

American students have always been told directly or indirectly that the major purpose of acquiring an education is to get a job. What better way to bring that message home than to start treating the acquiring of an education in just those terms, by paying students to attend school? There could be a sliding pay scale which would pay students who get higher grades more than those who achieve less, the same way a more skilled worker would command higher wages in the job market. On the other hand, under this system, any student could benefit monetarily from going to school, not just those who are college bound. ◉

Writing in the Workplace

Letter Writing

Workplace Writing: The Big Picture

Writing is a common workplace activity. Why? Because workers use letters, memos, and other documents as tools to communicate and do their work.

REVIEW & REACT: Check out the "Workplace Writing" section in your handbook (181-184). Pull together the ideas found there by answering the following questions:

1. What are the advantages of a "written message"?

2. Why do people write in the workplace?

3. What are the main types of workplace writing?

4. Look over the list of letters at the top of 183. Have you ever written or received one of these letters? Why did you write it or why was it sent?

5. According to the "Quick Guide" (184), what seven characteristics are shared by all types of workplace writing?

Letter-Writing Basics

Signed, sealed, and delivered—piles of letters whiz through the postal system far faster than anyone could have imagined even a few years ago. In fact, the U.S. Postal Service handles over 500 million pieces of mail each day. Why? Because businesses, nonprofit organizations, government offices—and people like you—write letters to get things done.

And what do real letters look like? A good way to find out is to ask some real people to give you copies of some real letters.

Collecting

Gather your letters from three sources:

1. Yourself. What business letters have you written or received?

2. Relatives. Ask them for copies of business letters they've received or sent.

3. A local business or organization. Explain who you are and what you need. Ask for copies of letters they've received or sent.

Examining

Once you've gathered your samples, spread them out on a table. Read them and answer the questions below. Support your answers by citing specific examples from your model letters.

1. List three things all these letters have in common.

2. List three reasons why people send business letters.

3. What are three differences between personal letters and workplace letters?

4. Out of your pile, choose the best one and the worst. List three strengths of an effective letter and three weaknesses of an ineffective one.

follow-up Choose a letter that calls for a reply. Imagine that the letter was written to you. Draft a response, creating all the details you need to support your answer.

Getting Started: Readers and Reasons

A letter can't happen without a writer. But it's equally true that it can't happen without a reader. Writing a letter always begins with thinking about why you are writing (your purpose) to a specific person or group (your audience).

Testing Out Some Models

1. Read through Ardith Lein's letter (189) in your handbook. What is the purpose of the letter? Does the letter accomplish this purpose? How?

2. How does Lein, the writer, treat Charlotte Williams, the reader? Point to two places where Lein shows respect for Williams.

3. Pull out one of the models you collected. Does the letter clearly define the writer's purpose and show respect for the reader? How?

Getting Organized

In order to communicate ideas and information, all letters must be carefully organized. The three-part letter described in "Effective Letter Organization" (190) will help you group your ideas when your write. Read that section and then define each of the parts below in your own words:

1. Situation:

2. Explanation:

3. Action:

follow-up Check out at least two model letters—one from the handbook and one you've gathered—to see if the writers use this three-part structure effectively.

Write to the Point

Every letter should follow four rules: (1) Be direct. (State the good news or main point early in the message.) (2) Be brief. (3) Be clear. (4) Be polite. The following message, though complete, doesn't follow the four rules. Read the message through first and then do the following:

1. Highlight or underline the main point of the message.
2. Cross through material that is beside the point.
3. Revise the message to make it direct, brief, clear, and polite.

Note: The body of the letter has been double-spaced to make it easier to mark up.

333 S. Figueroa St.
Los Angeles, CA 90071-1000
September 19, 1995

Publicity Director
Warner Brothers Studios
4000 Warner Blvd.
Burbank, CA 91522-0001

Dear Publicity Director:

I love movies, and especially love the movies your studio puts out on a regular basis, each year. In the last couple of years I've just gotten a whole lot of pleasure and enjoyment from such proud productions as <u>Disclosure</u>, <u>Fatherland</u>, and <u>Interview with the Vampire</u>. Of course, they're just pulp entertainment but a great way to blow a couple of spare hours.

Allow me to introduce myself as a person. I am a student at Lincoln Heights High School and the co-chair of our 1996 Arts Fall Fund-Raising Auction, which will take place in the spring sometime. That makes me an important person at the school. The arts are a dynamic part of student life at LHHS. This year we've had as students the character-shaping opportunities to participate in a film club, drama productions, creative writing workshops, a community artist program, not to mention bands, orchestra, choirs, and other singing groups. That's a lot of stuff involving a lot of time and effort, and I don't have to tell you how important the arts are! Were it not for the concerted efforts of faculty, students, and generous bigshots like yourself, our arts program would be nonexistent.

The costs of instruments, video equipment, art supplies, uniforms, and field trips add up quickly, especially when many of our school's students come from families already struggling close to the poverty line. Would you be willing to donate three or four items of movie memorabilia to auction at our fund-raiser to be held some time in September? Believe me, such stuff would sell like hotcakes!

Needless to say, your donation would be in good company. At this time, we have already received some excellent items from Universal, Disney, MGM, Paramount, Tri-Star, and the Children's Television Workshop. I'd like to take this opportunity to "zoom in" and "focus" your attention on this issue in order to make this the most artistic year ever for Lincoln Heights High School. Your nonparticipation would obviously be a black mark on your studio's reputation.

Thank you for your time and consideration. If you have any questions or comments, please do not hesitate to contact me.

Yours sincerely,

Pablo Wargogh

The Write Look

A good host at a party is practical and polite. Before the party she smiles, greets you, takes your coat, and introduces you to others. After the party she returns your coat, thanks you for coming, and says good-bye.

THINK about it—a good letter is also practical and polite. Explain below what polite or practical purpose each part might serve for writer and reader. Refer to 187-189 in your handbook.

- Heading

- Inside Address

- Salutation

- Complimentary Closing

- Signature

- Initials

- Enclosure (Encl.)

- Copies (cc.)

PULL OUT one of your letter models and examine the format and presentation closely. Answer these questions.

1. Label the format as "full block," "semi-block," or "other." Is the format correct and consistent from start to finish? Would you change something? What? Why?

2. Label the parts of the letter. Are the necessary parts there? Are they correct? Does anything need fixing?

3. Is the letter presented effectively? (Look at margins and white space, centering on the page, clarity of the type, quality of the paper, typos.)

4. Does the letter communicate the information politely and give a positive impression of the writer?

Writing the Informative Letter

READ & REACT: Read the model "Informative Letter" (196 in your handbook) and the editor's four comments on the left side of the page: (1) **purpose** is clear, (2) **details** are reader-friendly, (3) **details** are complete and accurate, and (4) **friendly close** anticipates action. Then read the letter below and mark where it includes each of these qualities.

WALLA WALLA State Bank

Walla Walla, Washington 99362-0259

August 20, 1995

Robert and Elizabeth Randolph
2456 Walnut St.
Walla Walla, WA 99362-0513

Dear Mr. and Mrs. Randolph:

I'm writing to let you know about a change in the way your property tax payments will be handled. Presently, the Walla Walla County courthouse mails your property tax statement to you, and then you bring it in to us. Beginning in September, this process will change as follows:

1. The county will mail your statement directly to the bank (on March 15 and September 15 each year).

2. We will then make the payment from your escrow account on April 1 and October 1.

3. By the middle of April and October, you will receive a copy of your property tax statement and verification of payment.

We believe that this procedure will be more convenient for you, as well as more efficient for us. If you have any questions or concerns about this change, please call me at 527-6328 between 9:00 a.m. and 5:00 p.m.

Sincerely,

Lavonne Wallace

Lavonne Wallace
Marketing Director

WRITE: Review the four guidelines in the boxes in section 195 in your handbook. Then practice these guidelines by drafting a letter in response to one of the options below. You may have to gather some information.

OPTION #1: You work for the Utah Jazz publicity office and have received a letter from Jenny "Sky" Smithers. (See "The Letter of Inquiry" at 194 in your handbook.) Write an informative response to Jenny's letter. (You may make up the necessary details.)

OPTION #2: You work in the convention office of a large hotel. Ms. Diane Brydon called to set up the annual convention of calliope players. (What's a calliope? Look it up.) Write a follow-up letter confirming reservations, indicating convention arrangements, outlining services, and stating the hotel's cancellation policy, among other things. (*Hint:* If you need help, interview a business manager or clerk at a local hotel.)

OPTION #3: You work in your city's planning offices and have been given the job of informing city residents about the new recycling program. Draft a letter to be received by all city residents. (*Hint:* For information about recycling programs, go to your library or interview your science teacher.)

OPTION #4: You are the service manager for an auto dealership, and you've just gotten off the phone with a customer who bought a used car. The customer wanted to know what maintenance the car will need during the next two years and what the services will cost. Put the details of your discussion in a letter so the customer will have a written record for her convenience. (*Hint:* For information, go to the owner's manual of a car—any car— or visit a local auto dealership and interview the service manager.)

Making Inquiries

Have you read any "Help Wanted" classified ads recently? If you have, you know that a help wanted ad is basically an inquiry from a person who is looking for something or someone.

REVIEW: People making inquiries in the workplace are also looking for something. Often, the inquiry is spoken in person or over the phone, but sometimes a letter, memo, or E-mail is better. Read the "Advantages of a Written Message" in your handbook (182) and list two reasons for choosing to write out an inquiry:

1.

2.

READ: Turn to "The Letter of Inquiry" (194) in your handbook. Read through the explanation and answer the following questions:

1. What questions must the letter writer ask himself or herself?

2. Did Jenny "Sky" Smithers ask herself the questions listed above? Support your answer by citing details in the letter.

follow-up Explore the models you've collected. Do you have an inquiry among them? If so, analyze how effective its detective work is. If not, take a model that seems to be a response to an inquiry letter and draft the original inquiry.

REVISE: The letter below is poorly written. Revise the letter so it is brief, clear, and polite.

Hint: Read the editor's four side notes beside Jenny Smither's letter (194). Make your revision so clear that an editor could cite the same four qualities in it.

The Pierre Centennial Committee
315 Main Ave. NE
Pierre, SD 57501-1321

12 June 1995

Ms. Jill Scheekoffelle
240 Rue de Bagette
Pierre, SD 57501-1440

Dear Ms. Scheekoffelle:

Yes, the centennial will soon be upon us. What a great time to be a citizen of Pierre! We will need all the help we can get to pull off these celebrations.

The committee likes music, and good music for the centennial is a must, don't you agree? We have heard from reliable sources that you have written many songs about Pierre and that they are quality stuff. While you're just a local artist, one of your songs might do. That's what we really want from you, a really good one that will tell the whole world who we are for the next 100 years.

Can you imagine and manage that for us? All citizens would repay you and be in your debt.

Yours sincerely,

James Grandebouche

James Grandebouche
Committee Chairperson

The Write Start

IMAGINE that you are in each of the three situations below. Then decide **(a)** whether it's best to phone, write, or fax, **(b)** what information you want from the person, and **(c)** how you would phrase the request in a sentence or two.

1. You have to do a research paper about the planet Venus, and you're wondering if you may visit the local university observatory and talk to an astronomer there.

   a.

   b.

   c.

2. You are applying for a job, and you would like your boss from last summer to write a recommendation.

   a.

   b.

   c.

3. Your family is going to the Ozarks on vacation, and you want to know what there is for family entertainment in that area.

   a.

   b.

   c.

Writing a Letter of Inquiry

EXERCISE your inquiring mind. With a partner, draft an inquiry letter for one of the situations below. Remember to do your detective work: think carefully about what information you need and what questions you want answered.

1. Your company just transferred you from New York to New Orleans. Write to a real estate company explaining your situation and your needs.

2. Your company's public relations office is selecting a worthy nonprofit organization to receive the company Christmas gift of $5,000. Write to a local nonprofit organization for information on the work it does.

3. As a worker in a personnel department, part of your job is to lower the costs of health insurance and absenteeism. Write an inquiry letter to a local hospital about their outreach or wellness program.

4. Your organization had a scare last summer: it was 60 miles from the epicenter of an earthquake. Write to a local disaster-relief office about evacuation procedures as well as first-aid training.

5. Being incredibly farsighted, you are thinking ahead to retirement. Write an inquiry to a local investment counselor for information on planning for your "golden" years.

6. You have been assigned to write a report on a small business in your community. Write a letter of inquiry to a local business owner.

7. Your company has a problem with unwanted pests. Write a letter to the United States Department of Agriculture (or an environmental agency) asking for accurate information on available pesticides.

8. As a young person with tremendous gumption, you want to start your own business (lawn maintenance, child care, catering, pet care, whatever). Write to your local chamber of commerce or to a local business person asking for information on how to get started.

9. Write an inquiry letter requesting information from a college, technical school, or training program you are thinking about enrolling in after high school.

---

follow-up → Take a classmate's inquiry letter and investigate the questions or issues raised. Then write a reply in the form of an informative letter. Turn to 195-196 in the handbook for an explanation and a model informative letter.

The Thank-You Letter

Saying thank you in the workplace is an important part of the day-to-day routine. Sometimes a simple handwritten note will do; other times, a formal typed letter will be more appropriate.

CHECK OUT: Turn to "The Thank-You Letter" in your handbook (200-201) and review the explanation and the model. Then read the letter below and tell how it meets the five guidelines for writing a good thank-you letter.

1. Be selective:

2. Be sincere:

3. Be prompt:

4. Be personal:

5. Be specific:

---

7 June 1996

Dear Ms. Griffin:

Thank you for hosting the 1995 Miracle Network Telethon on June 4. Because of your hard work, this year's telethon topped the anticipated goal by more than $500,000!

Everyone on the committee appreciates the time you gave, your professional behavior on-screen under tiring conditions, and your enthusiasm for the cause of healing children. We all enjoyed, as well, your sense of humor. You helped make a long day seem shorter.

I wish you well in your daily work, and I also look forward to future work together on this important cause.

Sincerely,

Reggie Filpot

Reggie Filpot
Miracle Network Committee Chair

WRITE: Try your hand at writing thank-you's by drafting a letter for one of the following situations. Create all the details you need to make the situation real.

OPTION #1: Look up "The Bad-News Letter" in your handbook (199) and read the letter from Seth Baccam to Gloria Patton. Take the role of Ms. Patton. Mr. Baccam has managed to find an insurance company that will offer you an economical policy. Thank him.

OPTION #2: Look up "Writing Short Reports" in your handbook (227-229). At the end of his model report, Eric Rowe tells Ms. Doriani that he sent a thank-you letter to Sandi Walker. Draft the thank-you letter based upon the report itself.

OPTION #3: Write a thank-you letter to one of the following: the person who gave you a great summer job, or the teacher or employer who acted as a reference.

OPTION #4: Imagine you are a manager. An alert employee discovered a computer virus in your company's network and destroyed the bug. Draft a memo to the employee (with copies for his or her immediate supervisor and employee file).

Writing to Get a Job

Preparing Your Résumé

Few things are more important than finding a job you can live with. One important tool for doing that is your résumé. In a sense, your résumé is a research project in which you match a description of yourself to potential jobs and employers.

READ: Turn to "The Résumé" (206-207) in your handbook. Read through the explanation, tips, and sample résumé.

GATHER: While that information is soaking in, gather some sample résumés. You can use one or more of these resources:

1. Relatives or other adults you know
2. A résumé handbook from the library
3. A résumé service (a company that writes résumés for a fee)

REACT: After studying the sample résumé and the handbook information, answer the following questions:

1. What is a résumé?

2. What is a résumé's purpose?

3. What information does a résumé contain?

4. How is that information organized and presented? Why is it done this way?

5. What is a job objective, and how should the rest of the résumé relate to it? (For example, how does all the information in Mila Celis's résumé connect with her job objective?)

CHOOSE: You need to make smart choices in order to write a strong résumé for your job search. Here are two simple activities to help you make those choices:

1. Decide which of the following items belong in your résumé. Check the appropriate box; then check the answers at the bottom of the page. How well did you do?

	yes	no	optional	
a.	☐	☐	☐	marital status
b.	☐	☐	☐	religion
c.	☐	☐	☐	height and weight
d.	☐	☐	☐	reason for leaving a job
e.	☐	☐	☐	age
f.	☐	☐	☐	number of children
g.	☐	☐	☐	health
h.	☐	☐	☐	political party
i.	☐	☐	☐	salary history or expectations
j.	☐	☐	☐	names of your references
k.	☐	☐	☐	phone number
l.	☐	☐	☐	awards you received
m.	☐	☐	☐	hobbies
n.	☐	☐	☐	important projects you completed
o.	☐	☐	☐	grade point average
p.	☐	☐	☐	skills learned in a part-time job
q.	☐	☐	☐	fringe benefits you would like
r.	☐	☐	☐	whether you prefer a male or female supervisor

2. Decide what you should do with your résumé. Check the best answer from each of the sets below:

a. ☐ Fill your résumé with as much information as possible.
    ☐ Be selective. Choose those details most clearly related to the job applied for.

b. ☐ Use headings, plenty of white space, etc., in presenting the information on your résumé.
    ☐ Use small print and small margins in order to get your résumé on a single page.

c. ☐ Have one standard résumé that you send to all employers.
    ☐ Tailor your résumé for each different position.

Answers: *a.* optional *b.* no *c.* no *d.* no *e.* no *f.* optional *g.* no *h.* optional *i.* no *j.* optional *k.* yes *l.* yes *m.* optional *n.* yes *o.* optional *p.* optional *q.* no *r.* no

Know Yourself

You may think you have little to offer an employer, but if you take the time to inventory your experiences, qualities, and skills, you'll be surprised.

BRAINSTORM: For starters, pick two activities you have done or are involved in now. These activities can be from school, work, hobbies, extracurricular activities, volunteer projects, or travel. What have you accomplished in these activities? Answer this question by exploring the following for each activity:

1. **Actions or events involved:** What exactly did you do? What steps did you follow?

2. **Skills learned or used:** Did you learn how to use a piece of equipment, run a software program, perform a task, work toward a goal? Skills can be manual, social, intellectual, organizational, artistic, and more. Think broadly.

3. **Results:** What were the outcomes of the activity? Did you solve a problem, build something, win an award, successfully complete a job assignment?

4. **Organizations or people involved:** Whom did you work for or with? Whom did you serve? What contacts did you make? What did you learn from others?

5. **Quantities:** Are there certain aspects of the activity that can be added up or computed? Did you serve 250 customers, perform 800 oil and lube jobs without a problem, teach 20 six-year-olds for a week at camp, have perfect attendance, earn an *A* or a *B?*

follow-up   Once you've analyzed your activities, look through what you've written. Make a list of related skills, personal qualities, and achievements that appear. Then write a brief report answering this question: What do I have to offer an employer?

Know Employers

Designing and redesigning your résumé depend on understanding what employers look for and need in an applicant. Considering the employer's perspective will help you get a job interview—the point of your résumé in the first place.

INVESTIGATE: One way to learn what employers want is to talk with them. Set up a pre-résumé fact-finding interview with an employer or a recruiter who reads résumés regularly. Discuss the following:

1. What the employer needs from employees—in general and for a specific job

2. What the employer looks for in job applicants

3. What the employer wants to see in a résumé

ANALYZE: You can learn a lot about employers and what they are looking for simply by analyzing the job ads they post in newspapers and on bulletin boards. Here are some points to look for when reading a job ad:

- The type and size of the company
- The products and services it offers
- The market it serves
- Its growth
- Its corporate philosophy or principles
- The specific requirements of the job advertised
- Conditions of employment

For example, read the ad below and explain what information the ad gives you about the employer and what he or she is seeking.

Biomedical Electronics Technician (BMET)

Elkhorn Medical Center, a progressive health care facility, is currently seeking applicants for this full-time position. This position requires an AAS degree in Biomedical Electronics or equivalent experience. Experience in a health care facility is preferred. EMC offers a competitive salary and excellent benefits. Send résumé with salary history to: Recruiter, Elkhorn Medical Center, 602 North Third Street, Elkhorn, WI 53121

EOE/M/F/V/H

Write Your Résumé

PLAN: Pull together all the information you need. (Check your old résumé if you have one, as well as career-related writing you've done in other SourceBook activities.) Make sure that you have all the important details in front of you.

DRAFT: Using this information, write a first draft of your master résumé (a résumé that could be used for any job). Here are some tips for specific sections:

1. **Personal Data:** Include your name, address, and phone number—enough for the employer to identify you and contact you.

2. **Job Objective:** For now, keep it general by indicating the type of position you are looking for (summer, part-time, full-time) and the type of job you want.

3. **Skills Summary:** Consider adding this section to your résumé. In it you list what you consider to be the key qualities and skills that you have to offer an employer: skilled at using desktop publishing software, strong communication skills, punctual, and so forth.

4. **Work Experience:** If you have had a job, list dates and duties but also your accomplishments. Be specific (how many customers served, how many lawns mowed, etc.).

5. **Education:** Go beyond courses and diplomas by listing specific important projects. Focus on extracurricular activities if they are closely related to your job objective.

6. **Other:** List volunteer activities, awards, hobbies—especially if they involve skills and responsibilities that could be transferred to the workplace.

REVISE: Once your résumé is nearly complete, get feedback from a few people—a classmate, a teacher, a guidance counselor, a parent, someone in the workplace. Then revise.

TAILOR: Now that you have your master résumé in order, you can work at tailoring it to specific jobs. Find ads for two jobs: a summer or part-time job, and a full-time job in your career area. Then revise your résumé twice—once for each ad. What should you revise? Consider the following:

● Job Objective: Use the language of the ad in your statement.

● Skills Summary: Select and rephrase those items most important to the specific job.

● Work Experience and Education: Decide which is most important and put that information first. Select details most important to the specific job.

Writing an Application Letter

When you apply for a job, your application letter is your all-important introduction to an employer. Before you write your letter, however, consider the following approaches:

● **Application Letter:** This letter usually stands by itself. In it, you give a complete summary of your qualifications.

● **Cover Letter:** This letter accompanies your résumé and highlights key parts of it.

● **Inquiry Letter:** This letter asks about possible job openings within the company.

Note: Whichever option you choose, remember that the letter's purpose is to sell yourself so that the employer will want to interview you. Be brief, but don't be bashful.

READ: Check out "The Letter of Application" (208-209) in your handbook. Read through the explanation and sample application letter. Then answer the following questions:

1. What should your application letter request?

2. What should you focus on in your application letter? What should you avoid?

3. After reading the Mila Celis sample application letter, describe specifically how she

● demonstrates a polite, professional attitude and tone.

● shows that she is aware of the job's specific requirements.

● stresses her qualifications without sounding like a braggart.

● makes it easy for the employer to call her about an interview.

PROOFREAD: Remember that the smallest error in an application letter may weaken your chance of getting an interview. Do you need some proofreading practice? Read and correct the application letter below. Refer to your handbook whenever you have questions about punctuation, usage, capitalization, etc. (Note: The letter is double-spaced to make it easier to correct.)

2461 Partridge Woods court
Lake Geneva Wi 53147
April 1, 1996

William Harris, d.v.m.
3322 W. State Street
Lake Geneva WI 53147

Dear Dr. Harris

I am very interested in the position of part-time vetranary assistant that you

advertised in the March 30 issue of the Lake Geneva regional news. I enjoy

working with animals and have worked at Cedardale kennels as a dog groomer for

the passed two summers. I've been a 4-H member since I was seven years old and

have won numerous awards in horsemanship. My parents own a dairy farm and

I have had alot of experience caring for calves, chickens and turkeys.

This semester I am participating in a work-study program for juniors at Badger

high school   the program allows students to attend school in the morning and work

in the afternoon. I finish classes every day at 11:00 a m and I am free to work

afternoons, evenings, and Saturdays. If you are looking for someone who really

cares for and has experience with animals please call me at 248-2121.

Sincerely

Sandy K. Miles

Sandy K. Miles

IMAGINE: If you were the person in the résumé below, and you wanted to apply for the job in the ad, what would you put in your application letter? Draft a cover letter for this situation.

DENTAL TECHNICIAN
Orthodontic Office

Full-time ortho assistant needed for modern 2-doctor practice. Position requires knowledge of orthodontic appliances and partial dentures, ability to assist with patients. Excellent wage, benefits, and bonus package. Send résumé to Wilkes and Waters Orthodontists, Medical Professional Building, Claymont, DE 19704.

DAWN NEIDICH
2301 Euclid Ave.
Claymont, DE 19703-4712
(215) 265-3889

JOB OBJECTIVE:

Full-time ortho assistant/technician in medium-sized orthodontist office.

SKILLS SUMMARY:

Strong manual dexterity skills, very precise and careful attention to procedures.

Perform many tasks efficiently, organize different duties, pay attention to details.
Skilled at making patients feel comfortable through talking, listening, and using sense of humor.

Work well independently, show initiative and ability to get work done on time.

EXPERIENCE:

Receptionist/Bookkeeper, Dr. Ken Ellis, D.D.S. Duties include typing, filing insurance, answering the phone, scheduling appointments, balancing the daysheet, making deposits, doing quarterly taxes. May 1993 to present.

Dental Assistant, Dr. Ken Ellis, D.D.S. Duties included cleaning teeth, sterilizing instruments, assisting dentist during procedures. June 1991 to May 1993.

EDUCATION AND TRAINING:

Removable Appliance Fabrication course. Great Lakes Orthodontist Lab, Buffalo, New York. Learned to diagnose study models and make removable appliances. Summer 1995.

X-Ray Certification course. Delaware Technical College. Learned about X-ray science, technology, and procedures, including dental X-rays. Fall 1994.

General Accounting degree. Western Technical College, Buffalo, New York. Course highlights: Accounting, Business Writing, Speech. Graduated 1990.

COMMUNITY INVOLVEMENT:

Volunteer Treasurer, Growing Tree Children's Center. Prepare weekly payroll, monthly balance sheets, and quarterly taxes. 1993 to present.

Requesting a Reference or Recommendation

When someone acts as a reference for you, he or she is saying that you are fit to do the work in whatever program, apprenticeship, or job you are applying for.

How do you get this fitness certificate? By doing good work for someone, of course, but also by writing a courteous and clear letter requesting that the person serve as a reference or write a recommendation.

READ: Turn to "The Request Letter" (205) in your handbook and read the explanation and model. Then answer the following questions:

1. In your own words, define the three parts of the request letter.

2. What kind of information should you include in the letter to make the reader's job of acting as a reference easier?

3. How would you describe the tone that Mila Celis uses in her letter? Why is that tone important?

CHOOSE: When you need a reference or recommendation, you have several choices to think through.

1. Whom should you choose as a reference? Teachers, employers, supervisors, coworkers, neighbors, clergy? Make a list of four or five people who could act as a reference or write a letter of recommendation for you.

2. You can't dictate what your reference says about you, but you can refresh his or her memory. What does this person know about you? Check out the SCANS competencies and foundational skills (449-452) for clues concerning the kind of information your reference could share.

REACT: Imagine that students wrote the following two request letters. Read each example from the teacher's point of view. Would you want to write a recommendation for Joe Buddy? Why or why not? What about Timothy Bartels? What are the key differences between the letters?

July 12, 1996

Miss or Mrs. Janet Nero
Physics teacher
Western Kentucky Technical College
Hopkinsville, KY 42240

Dear Janet:

How's it goin? Things are pretty hot here, but I'm surviving. I hope you are too. Are you still teaching physics? You were my favorite teacher at WKTC.

I was in your physics class about six years ago or thereabouts. I dropped out but I'm thinking of going back to school at Lexington Technical College. I'm writing this letter to ask if you would please, please write a letter of recommendation for me? I'd appreciate it a great deal! Thanks!

Your affectionate past student,

Joe Buddy

Joe Buddy

---

55 Cottage Grove Lane
Cary, MS 39054
March 3, 1996

Ms. Gail Scott
Electronics Teacher
Leacock High School
Cary, MS 39054

Dear Ms. Scott:

As a senior, I've begun applying to colleges that offer electronics and electrical engineering programs. Because you encouraged me to pursue, as you called it, "a shocking career in electricity," I'm writing to ask if you would write a letter recommending me to the electrical engineering program at Hattiesburg Technical College.

As you may recall, in your Advanced Electronics class, 1993-94, I consistently received A's on my projects and tests. You remarked on my term project that I had a strong grasp of both electronics principles and the hands-on design of circuit systems.

The deadline for recommendations is April 10, 1996, and the person to address is Professor Charles Reisman, electrical engineering program coordinator. I've enclosed a pre-addressed, stamped envelope for your convenience. Please call me at 278-8549 if you need further information. Your recommendation to the program will mean a lot because you have closely observed my work in electronics.

Sincerely,

Timothy Bartels

Timothy Bartels

WRITE: You need three references for a summer, part-time, or entry-level job application. Write a letter of request to one of the three people you might actually ask. You might find it helpful to start with real job ads and program descriptions. (Check your local newspaper.)

Filling Out Application Forms

Sometimes applying for a job feels like taking a test—especially when you're staring at a lengthy application form. The form may be the first (and last) impression you make on an employer, so it's worth learning to get it right.

READ: Turn to "The Application Form" (203-204) in your handbook and read through the page. Put in your own words the main point behind all the advice in the "Quick Guide."

RESEARCH: By doing some research, you can better understand the role of application forms in your job search.

1. Check out the form on the next two pages and draw some conclusions about what employers want from forms. What kind of information is requested? How are questions organized (what kind of information is asked for first, second, and so on)? How much space is given for answers?

2. Interview someone in the workplace who reads applications. Get his or her perspective by asking questions like these:

● Why do you use application forms? Why not just collect résumés from people?

● What are you looking for in an application form? What makes you look positively or negatively at a completed application? What screening process do you use?

WRITE: Find an ad for a job you might be interested in. Then fill out the form on the following two pages as if you were applying for the job.

APPLICATION FOR EMPLOYMENT

(PLEASE PRINT)

DATE OF APPLICATION

NAME
LAST   FIRST   MIDDLE

PRESENT ADDRESS
STREET   CITY   STATE   ZIP

TELEPHONE (   )
AREA CODE

SOCIAL SECURITY NUMBER

What Days Are You NOT Available to Work?

What Hours Are You NOT Available to Work? (AM or PM)   ☐ MON ☐ TUE ☐ WED ☐ THURS ☐ FRI ☐ SAT ☐ SUN

Please indicate which types of employment interest you (check more than one box if you wish):

☐ Permanent (Full-Time) ☐ Permanent (Part-Time) ☐ Temporary (Full-Time) until   ☐ Temporary (Part-Time) until

	YES	NO
1) Do you have access to a car (for some positions, a vehicle is required)?	☐ YES	☐ NO
2) Do you have a valid driver's license?	☐ YES	☐ NO
3) Are you over age 18?	☐ YES	☐ NO
4) Are you a U.S. citizen or do you have an entry permit that allows you to work?	☐ YES	☐ NO

EMPLOYMENT DESIRED

POSITION

DATE YOU
CAN START

SALARY
DESIRED

ARE YOU EMPLOYED NOW?

IF SO, MAY WE COMMUNICATE
WITH YOUR PRESENT EMPLOYER?

WILL YOU WORK OVERTIME IF ASKED?

EVER APPLIED TO THIS COMPANY BEFORE?   WHEN?

EDUCATION	NAME AND LOCATION OF SCHOOL	NO. YRS. ATTENDED	DID YOU GRADUATE?	DEGREE AND MAJOR
Elementary School				
High School				
College				
Trade, Business, or Correspondence School				

VETERAN OF U.S. MILITARY SERVICE?   IF YES, BRANCH

PERIOD OF ACTIVE DUTY: FROM   TO   DUTIES

PRESENT MEMBERSHIP IN
NATIONAL GUARD OR RESERVES?

ACTIVITIES OTHER THAN RELIGIOUS
(SCHOOL, COMMUNITY, ATHLETIC, ETC.)

Exclude organizations the name or character of which indicates the race, creed, color, or national origin of its members.

(CONTINUED ON OTHER SIDE)

For some positions, it may be required that employees possess certain physical capabilities. Check the appropriate boxes below that you feel reflect the physical activities in which you can routinely engage without harm to yourself or fellow employees. Please be assured that a negative answer will NOT disqualify you from consideration.

1) Lifting: ☐ 25 lbs. or less ☐ 75 lbs.
☐ 50 lbs. ☐ 100 lbs. or more

2) Do You Have Difficulties: ☐ Bending? ☐ Standing for long periods of time?
☐ Climbing? ☐ Working in temperature extremes?

3) List any physical limitations that you feel may relate to the work for which you are applying:

_____

_____

4) Have you been convicted of any violations other than minor traffic violations? ☐ YES ☐ NO

5) If yes, of what were you convicted, when, and where?

_____

_____

WORK EXPERIENCE Provide a complete description. This information will be used to determine if your application is accepted. Be specific. Start with your most recent job. For part-time work, show the average number of hours per month. Indicate any changes in job title under same employer as a separate position. You may also attach a separate sheet with additional information.

Employer	Kind of Business	Location (Numbered Street)
Your Title	Reason for Leaving	Location (City, State, ZIP)
Your Duties:		Name of Supervisor:

Total Time Employed:	Check one:	Full-Time Part-Time (___ hrs./mo.)
From (Month & Year)		To (Month & Year)

Check one:
Monthly Salary   Beginning: $
Hourly Salary   Ending: $

Employer	Kind of Business	Location (Numbered Street)
Your Title	Reason for Leaving	Location (City, State, ZIP)
Your Duties:		Name of Supervisor:

Total Time Employed:	Check one:	Full-Time Part-Time (___ hrs./mo.)
From (Month & Year)		To (Month & Year)

Check one:
Monthly Salary   Beginning: $
Hourly Salary   Ending: $

REFERENCES

NAME _____ ADDRESS _____ PHONE _____

NAME _____ ADDRESS _____ PHONE _____

NAME _____ ADDRESS _____ PHONE _____

Creating a Career Plan
What Is a Career?

When I was young, my parents' idea of a good time was to take us kids for a drive in the country. Sometimes I'd ask my dad where we were going, and he'd answer, "I'm following my nose."

Where are you going and how are you getting there? Are you *following* your nose, *being led* by the nose, or *pointing* your nose in the right direction? Where will you be and what will you be doing when you're 20, 40, or 60 years old? These are tough questions worth thinking about.

IMAGINE: Take a minute to think about who you are and what you want to be in the future. Imagine where you want to be and what you want to be doing. Answer one of the following questions. (Use your own paper.)

1. Choose one age anywhere between 30 and 70 and provide a detailed portrait of yourself.

2. Choose four well-spaced ages between 20 and 70 and provide a brief snapshot of yourself for each.

READ: How does a career fit into your future? Read these sections in your handbook: "Preparing for the Workplace" (444-446) and "Preparing for Changes in the Workplace" (449-452). Then, on your own paper, answer the questions below.

1. Based on your reading of sections 444-446, summarize how the workplace is changing.

2. What career would you like to pursue? Cite three ways in which you think that career has changed in the last ten years.

3. Review the "basic competencies" in sections 450-451. Which ones will you need in your career?

4. Review the "foundational skills" in section 452. Which of these will you use in your career?

INSIDE
info

In today's and tomorrow's workplace, workers will frequently change directions in their careers and training. How should that affect your career plan? Plan for change by

● thinking broadly about what you like to do and could do,
● getting an education that teaches up-to-date skills, and
● planning to update your education throughout your career.

A Personal Inventory

Perhaps you've already visited your guidance counselor and taken tests to figure out your interests and skills. Consider what you learned and use that insight to do the following personal writing.

THINK: After reflecting for a while, answer the questions below.

1. Brainstorm a list of your strengths as a person. What are you good at and what do you enjoy?

2. Based on your brainstorming above, make a list of five occupations you think you would enjoy and be good at. (Consider making your list with the help of an occupational reference work. You should be able to find several in your school library.)

EXPLORE: What work have you done or are you doing? Maybe you've had a summer job. Maybe you have a part-time job now. Or maybe you're responsible for chores at home or extracurricular duties at school. Think about your work:

1. List specific jobs or duties you've been assigned. Then briefly explain how you go about doing them successfully.

2. What do you expect to gain from your work?

3. What does your employer expect from you?

4. What do clients or customers expect of you?

5. What does the word "work" mean?

Career Research

Perhaps, by now, you have a few career options in mind. To make final decisions, you'll need to explore these options further.

INTERVIEW: Do you know someone in an interesting career? Set up an interview to talk about the nature of that occupation. Review "Conducting Interviews" (341-344) in your handbook. Write a summary of your interview to share in class.

OBSERVE: You can learn a lot by observing a person at work. "Shadow" a worker for a couple of hours or a day (with permission, of course). Then write up a report on that career to share in class. Check out Eric Rowe's "Model Short Report" (228-229).

WRITE: Build on the research you've already done to write a report on a specific career area. Consult the Department of Labor's *Occupational Outlook Handbook* and talk to your guidance counselor.

The report may include the following:

1. A description of the career area or specific occupations

2. An explanation of your interest in the career

3. An explanation of how to prepare for the career

4. An evaluation of the positives and negatives of this career, its suitability to you, and its future

The SCANS Report Card

How well are you preparing yourself for a career? First, study "Foundational Skills" (452 in your handbook). These are skills that business people want all their employees to have. Then measure your progress toward achieving the skills by filling out the SCANS Progress Report below. (The *SCANS Report* was written by a group of leaders in business, industry, and education to help students prepare for the workplace.)

Basic Skills	Excellent	Average	Poor	Not Sure
Reading				
Writing				
Arithmetic/Mathematics				
Listening				
Speaking				
Thinking Skills				
Creative Thinking				
Decision Making				
Problem Solving				
Knowing How to Learn				
Reasoning				
Personal Qualities				
Responsibility				
Self-Esteem				
Self-Management				
Integrity/Honesty				

READ & REACT: Read "Preparing for Changes in the Workplace" and "Basic Competencies" (449-451 in your handbook). Business leaders from across the country say that

● all employees in the workplace need the competencies on these two pages.
● all the competencies are based on the skills in your Progress Report above!

What do you feel are your greatest strengths and weaknesses? How can you go about improving upon your weaknesses?

Drafting a Career Plan

All of us have goals—even if we don't think about them. Pulling through an illness or a tough week of exams, making the team, finding a summer job—each of these is related to a goal, whether or not it's stated.

We have a better chance of reaching our goals, however, if they are plain to see—carefully chosen, tested, and planned out.

DREAM: Turn to "Setting Goals" (460-462) in your handbook and review the explanation of primary and secondary goals. Then brainstorm a list of primary goals for your life. (You could include areas like career, family, or lifestyle.) Choose one primary goal and develop a set of secondary goals to reach it. Include some concrete steps between your present situation and your long-range goals.

Primary Goals: ....

....

....

One Primary Goal: ....

    Secondary Goals: ....

    ....

    ....

    ....

READ & REACT: Once you have goals in mind, you are close to developing a career plan. This plan is like a map: it gives you a destination and shows you how to get there. Read "Planning a Career" (463-464) in your handbook. Based on your reading, evaluate the career plan on the next two pages by answering these questions:

1. Is this plan realistic?

2. What different paths does the plan provide to get to the destination or goal?

Career Plan

Personal Data

Eric Rowe
498 Fourth Ave. NE
Hobart, Ohio 45013-2199

Career Field and Specific Jobs

I'm interested in recreation occupations. Why? Because this career field will allow me to use my strengths in athletics, organization, and working with people. Recreation workers help all types of people enjoy their leisure time, and I think I'd like doing this.

Rec workers run many programs: sports and fitness activities, camping, wellness programs, arts and crafts, wildlife work, and social events. And rec workers get to work in many places: amusement parks, fitness centers, cruise ships, public parks, pools, hotels, the military, nursing homes, playgrounds, businesses, and industries.

Some Specific Jobs in Recreation

recreation director or supervisor	wellness director
recreation aide	exercise specialist
social director	camp counselor or director

Degrees or Certification Needed

I can enter the recreation field with a high-school degree, but moving up requires a degree from a two-year or four-year college. I should take a college program in arts and recreation, physical education, leisure studies, parks and recreation management, or fitness management.

I should also get certified in certain sports and CPR. It's most important that I get professional certification from the National Recreation and Park Association (NRPA).

Certified Leisure Technician (CLT)—two-year college grads

Certified Leisure Professional (CLP)—four-year college grads

If I pursue wellness director or exercise specialist, I should also get certification for fitness instructors from the American College of Sports Medicine. Possible colleges with Leisure Studies programs: Hobart Community College, Northwest Ohio Technical College, Ohio State University, Wooster College.

Useful Work Experiences

Recreation jobs involve working with people in physical and social activities, so my work experiences should include these:

Part-time or summer jobs: pool lifeguard, camp counselor, worker in a public park or amusement park, referee for city intramural sports, fitness center employee

Internships: park or wellness program

Volunteer work: senior citizens, children, or other teens (Big Brother, YMCA, volunteer coach, senior Tai Kwon Do)

My Past Accomplishments

While I haven't yet done a lot of recreation work, I've made a good start.

Courses taken: physical education, theater, office practices, applied communications, sociology, psychology, physiology

Extracurricular activities: AWOL visit with Hobart rec director Sandi Walker; basketball and track teams; Break-a-Leg Drama Club

Work experiences: Hobart Basketball Camp worker (summer '93), Big Lake Youth Camp counselor (summer '94 and '95)

Awards: First place in the 100-yard freestyle at the Tri-Center Swim Meet, honorable mention on State 2A basketball team

Certifications: Red Cross First Aid, Red Cross Lifeguard Training, Youth Leadership Seminar

People or Organizations That Could Help Me

I think that there are several people and organizations that can help me get my foot in the "recreation career door."

People: Aunt Jackie Williams (city recreation office), Jim Burrows (high-school guidance counselor), Coach Appleby (swim team), Marlene Ronco (youth camp director)

Organizations: Hobart Fitness Club, the American Association for Leisure and Recreation (AALR), the National Recreation and Park Association (NRPA), the American Camping Association (ACA), the American College of Sports Medicine (ACSM)

Plan-of-Action

If I take the following steps, my rec career should be on the right track.

1. Finish high school. Keep focusing on courses in physical education, business, communications, English, science courses that look at the human body and nutrition, social science courses dealing with community and psychology. Continue in sports, drama, and music extracurricular activities. Apply for a work-study internship.

2. Look into colleges. Contact 2-year and 4-year colleges for information on Leisure Studies programs. Discuss options with Mr. Burrows.

3. Keep up recreation-related work. Continue as camp counselor, look for part-time or volunteer work to do during school year. Contact Aunt Jackie and others.

4. Check out certification process. Look into local CPR and lifesaving classes. Contact AALR, NRPA, and ACSM for info on recreation careers and student memberships.

Writing on the Job

Writing Memos—The Big Picture

What are memos? Why do people write and read them? Why not just use the phone? What's in a memo, anyway? With these questions in mind, **READ** the following memo:

Date: 20 July 1995
To: Zachariah Zanzibub
From: Carlotta Johnson
Subject: New Copy Machine Code Number

The new Xerox 5034 copy machine will be installed tomorrow. This machine will keep track of copies through a computerized counter that automatically charges the appropriate department based on a code punched into the machine. You need to do the following before the machine is installed:

1. Check how many copies are left on the copy card you used in the old machine. Then turn in the card to me along with that number. I will credit your department with the proper number of copies.

2. Memorize the following new code number for your department: 1527. Please do not let anyone else know your number. (Don't even mention it in your sleep.)

At 3:00 p.m. next Wednesday, Alley Franklin will demonstrate the new copier's features to all engineering staff.

REACT: Why was this memo written? In other words, (1) how does it help the reader, and (2) what does it expect of the reader?

REFLECT: Turn to "Writing Memos" (215) in your handbook. With Carlotta's memo fresh in your mind, read through the explanation of memos and the model. Then answer these questions:

1. Why are memos written?

2. What are three important things to do when you write a memo?

REVISE: Always give yourself time for revision. Coworkers are annoyed by memos that aren't clear or don't get to the point. This problem becomes even worse with E-mail, when, too often, people dash off messages without revision. Revise the memo below so that it looks and sounds both clear and professional. (Use the Inter-Tech, Inc. memo, 215, as your model.)

Date: Aug. 5/95 to Jerry "Mr. Clean" Brummer in Maint. about cleanliness next to godliness

Heh, Jerry! Great softball game last night! Thanks to your great pitching, our team might be respectable come end of the season. Speaking of softball, have you been busy with maintenance these days? The dumpster outside my window is overflowing and kind of stinky. If you don't move it, I'll have to personally report you to the fresh air council and break all of your pitching fingers.

Your friend,
Shirley "I'm no angel" Angelina

Writing Personal Memos

WRITE: Using what you've learned, draft a memo for one of the situations below. (Start by thinking about who your reader is and what you want your memo to accomplish.)

OPTION #1: Your birthday is rapidly approaching. Write a memo reminding one of the following of this joyous event (and your expectations): an adult relative, a parent, brother, sister, cousin, or friend.

OPTION #2: Your sister or brother is constantly borrowing your clothes without asking. Write a memo reminding your sibling of the location of his or her own closet and the penalties associated with borrowing without permission.

OPTION #3: You are hosting a video party Friday night, and you are concerned about the stock of edibles in the kitchen. Write a memo to your parents about the importance of food to your social life.

Writing Business Memos 1

WRITE: Now that you have practiced writing a personal memo, you are ready for a major league memo. Below you will find a number of options. Choose one and write a memo that would result in effective workplace communication.

OPTION #1: You are Ardith Lein, the executive director of the Savannah Chamber of Commerce who wrote to Charlotte Williams in "Form of the Business Letter" (189). Charlotte agreed to join the chamber of commerce and wants a ribbon-cutting ceremony. Make up necessary details and write a memo to chamber members about the upcoming ceremony.

OPTION #2: You are Ardith Lein, the executive director of the Savannah Chamber of Commerce. Write a memo to a chamber member informing her or him that she or he has been appointed to the Picnic and Program Committee for the coming year.

OPTION #3: You are Gene Ebert from the Public Relations Office of the Utah Jazz. You have received Jenny "Sky" Smithers' request (see "The Letter of Inquiry," 194). You believe that the visit from Jenny's crew might be a good photo opportunity. Write a memo about it to the coach of the Cedar City Crusaders.

Writing Business Memos 2

WRITE: Do you want MORE options still? Try out one of the following "put yourself in my shoes" situations. You may have to do a little workplace research to make these memos effective. Write your memo on your own paper or computer.

OPTION #1: You are the head of maintenance for a large hotel. Write a memo about the annual pool cleaning to one of the following people: maintenance staff, recreation director, hotel manager, head of security, customer relations manager.

OPTION #2: You are the manager of a travel agency. Write a memo to all staff about a new tour package.

OPTION #3: You head up the sales staff for a company that manufactures graphics software. Write a memo to all sales staff concerning a new software program from your company that's ready for the market.

OPTION #4: You are a social worker specializing in domestic violence cases. Write a memo to your supervisor about a particularly difficult case. Request a meeting to discuss it.

OPTION #5: You work in the business office of a sports equipment distributor. Write a memo to all employees about direct deposit paychecks and the company's plans to implement such a program as a cost-effective and convenient practice.

Writing Bulletins—or, Public Memos

"Put out an APB: young male, approximately 18, 5'11", 145 lbs." We've all heard words similar to these on cop shows, but an "APB"? What is it? It's an **all-p**oints **b**ulletin—a message sent to all police stations, cruisers, and foot patrols.

A bulletin is an APB to the people you are trying to reach—coworkers, customers, neighbors, whomever. This section of your SourceBook will help you learn to use bulletins effectively.

RESEARCH: Public memos are all around us. Search your school and community for some bulletin boards. Check out the counselor's office, a grocery store, a library, a mall, a post office, a computer network. Look first at the overall bulletin board and the general size and shape of what's on it. Then scan the individual messages and answer the questions below:

1. Where exactly are these bulletin boards located? Why is location important?

2. What are some topics that bulletins cover?

3. Do you see any bulletins that are good, poor, bizarre, or funny? Record them so that you can share them with classmates.

4. What is a bulletin? Write a single-sentence definition. Then check out a dictionary's definition.

SHARE: Return to class with your answers. Discuss with classmates what you discovered about bulletins.

● Consider that bulletins may be intended for a handful of people or for millions.
● Think of computer bulletin boards on the Internet.
● Talk about why details are important and how bulletins are similar to memos.

READ: Imagine that the bulletin below is posted beside the employee time cards in a restaurant. Read it (on an empty stomach).

All Employees: Please Read Carefully!

Diners don't consider cockroaches appropriate dining companions. For this reason, Jerry's Cafe now has a cockroach prevention and control program. Here's what you need to know:

1. Chemical sprays will be a last resort.

2. Instead, cockroaches will be attacked three ways: habitat modification, sanitation, and nontoxic controls (sticky traps, diatomite filters, boric acid).

Employee responsibilities will be sanitation and customer relations:

1. Keep the dining and kitchen areas clean during the day and sanitized at night:

    a. Clean up all food and drink spills immediately.
    b. Keep food covered and stored in sealed containers.
    c. Clean around, beneath, and behind appliances, sinks, and other dark, damp places.
    d. Take out garbage several times each day and clean the garbage cans and areas daily.
    e. Vacuum the dining area twice per day to remove food particles.

2. If a cockroach appears in the dining area, please handle it (the situation, not the cockroach) delicately:

    a. Avoid screaming, stomping on the bug, and other unprofessional behavior.
    b. Do apologize sincerely, remove the customers' food immediately, and offer them a free meal or a rain check.
    c. Once the situation has been handled, report the sighting to your supervisor.

REACT: Think about the delicacy of the situation and answer these questions:

1. Why would this bulletin be posted where it is?

2. What is the main point of this bulletin? Why was it written, and for whom?

3. Do you think this bulletin works well? Why?

Writing Well-Worded Bulletins

READ the following bulletin. Notice the authoritarian, heavy-handed way the bulletin is written. It is not at all friendly or respectful of the employees. See if you agree that this bulletin would most likely cause more problems than it would solve.

Like a Rock Insurance Brokers

BULLETIN—PAY ATTENTION

In accordance with managerial policies established with due consideration, each and every, to wit, ALL Like a Rock employees are hereby notified of the following changes to this company's dress code:

1. NO EMPLOYEE of this company shall wear foot apparel of the tennis-playing variety.

2. NO EMPLOYEE of this company shall appear on the premises appareled in clothing commonly referred to as "blue jeans," whether the coloration of this material be blue, black, white, green, or any other color revealed through spectrum analysis.

3. NO FEMALE EMPLOYEE of this company shall report to her position in skirts or dresses more than 2.5 inches above the knee.

4. NO MALE EMPLOYEE of this company shall report to his position in a nonwhite shirt—not even off-white. It goes without saying that a tie is mandatory, but all ties deemed eccentric will be duly removed from the neck and replaced. All ties must be tied with a company "stranglehold" knot.

COMPLIANCE IS MANDATORY.

REVISE the bulletin above by doing the following:

1. In your handbook turn to the table "Expressions to Avoid in Workplace Writing," 185. Review the examples under "Formal and Awkward Phrasing." These are just a few of the many awkward, indirect phrases that can crop up in business writing.

2. Highlight or underline formal or awkward phrasing in the bulletin.

3. Revise the whole message to improve the tone. (Hint: People are more likely to agree if you give reasons.)

Writing Bulletins

WRITE: Now it's your turn to write a bulletin. Before you get to the options below, however, turn to "Writing Memos" in your handbook (215) to review the qualities of all good memos including bulletins. For some of the options below, you may have to do some personal research to gather details.

OPTION #1: You work in a high-tech company that thrives on retooling and upgrading employee knowledge and skills. Write a bulletin about a specific course available to employees.

OPTION #2: The specialty seafood shop you manage is changing its hours in response to a customer survey. Inform potentially "crabby" employees of the changes.

OPTION #3: You are a nursing supervisor in the trauma ward of a large hospital. Write a bulletin to inform people about safe areas in the event of a tornado. The bulletin will be posted in the waiting area for patients, family, and friends.

Bulletin

Messages: Leaving, Taking, Giving

The camera frames Roberto, a secretary, writing down a phone message for Angie, a detective who's in the washroom feeling sick after seeing her first corpse. The message is from Rosco, an informant, and reads, "I know who killed Bubba. Meet me at the Pizza Ranch at 11 tonight." Roberto places the message on Angie's desk and leaves. Just before Angie returns, a breeze from the window ruffles papers on the desk and sweeps the message into the wastebasket.

You know the rest. Rosco's dead at 11:05 p.m. TV shows and movies often use the missed, lost, or found message as a plot device—the information changes characters' lives.

In the workplace, messages also affect lives—of coworkers, customers, and clients. Giving and relaying messages is crucial to workplace communication.

REVIEW: Turn to "Telephone Etiquette" (216) and "Writing Telephone Messages" (217) in your handbook. After reading these sections, respond to the following questions:

1. How does telephone etiquette help you give and take messages effectively?

2. Why is it important to take messages carefully and deliver them promptly? What are some of the potential problems of not being clear or prompt?

3. What are five important elements to be included in a telephone message?

4. What experiences have you had with phone messages at home or at work? Do they always work smoothly? Why or why not? Think of an example from your experience.

follow-up Share your answers with two classmates. What agreement can you reach on each question?

Talk to the Experts

In order to understand how messages function in the workplace, you need to get some feedback from a message taker. Review "Conducting Interviews" (341-344) in your handbook. Then telephone a local company, nonprofit organization, or government office. Follow this procedure:

1. Introduce yourself, explain your purpose in calling, and ask if the listener or another employee has a few moments to answer your questions about messages. Make sure you get and record the person's name and position accurately.

2. Ask a series of questions that you have developed or that occur to you as you converse with the person, or use the questions below:

   a. What types of messages do you have to take down?

   b. What do you do to get the message right?

   c. How do you get the message to the right person?

   d. Have you ever had to take a really strange or funny message?

   e. Have you ever taken a message from an impolite caller? What did you do in that situation?

   f. Do you have any advice on how to make messages work?

3. Thank the person for helping you with your project.

---

follow-up Bring your interview notes to class and discuss with two classmates what you discovered about messages in the workplace. Based on your discussion, work together to draft a memo in which you advise others how to make messages work.

Writing Effective Messages

Message receivers need the full facts to respond well to a message. You, the message writer, provide the full facts by

1. answering the five W's and
2. avoiding ambiguity.

DEFINE: Look up "Ambiguous wording" in your handbook index. Check it out and define "ambiguity" below:

Ambiguity is ....

READ & REACT: With this understanding of ambiguity in mind, work through the two versions of the message that follow.

● Read the first version and highlight or circle all portions that are unclear or ambiguous.

The Body Shop Fitness Center
IMPORTANT MESSAGE

TO *Personnel*

DATE *this Morning*

FROM *Arty of L. and B. sporting (goods?)—I think*

PHONE

Telephoned	✔	Please Call	✔
Came to See You		Will Call Again	✔
Returned Your Call	✔	Special Attention	

MESSAGE *This guy Arty called about LB sports goods about a guy he knows in California somewhere. He says he's got the stuff you're looking for—some stairs and a rowboat. He also mentioned that thing by Suzanne Winters. They sounded kind of shifty to me, but you know best I suppose.*

SIGNED *Q*

```
┌─────────────────────────────────────────┐
│  ┌────────────────────────────────────┐  │
│  │   The Body Shop Fitness Center     │  │
│  │        IMPORTANT MESSAGE           │  │
│  │                                    │  │
│  │  TO  Reba McLeod                   │  │
│  │                                    │  │
│  │  DATE  6/16/96  10:45 a.m.         │  │
│  │                                    │  │
│  │  FROM  Arthur Laucaster of L&B     │  │
│  │        Sporting Goods              │  │
│  │                                    │  │
│  │  PHONE  1-555-453-1422             │  │
│  └────────────────────────────────────┘  │
└─────────────────────────────────────────┘
```

The Body Shop Fitness Center
IMPORTANT MESSAGE

TO Reba McLeod

DATE 6/16/96 10:45 a.m.

FROM Arthur Laucaster of L & B Sporting Goods

PHONE 1-555-453-1422

Telephoned		Please Call	✔
Came to See You		Will Call Again	
Returned Your Call	✔	Special Attention	

MESSAGE Mr. Laucaster knows someone from San Diego who can supply the stair climber ($329) and rowing machine ($399) you're looking for. The man's name is Bicepy Brawnsky, and his number is 1-555-453-1422. Brawnsky also has a warehouse full of Thighmasters if you're interested in a couple.

SIGNED Alexis Coral

● Now read the second version, and highlight or list the key differences.

WRITE: Use your understanding of messages to create your own for one of the following situations. You must develop the details needed. Use blank paper, message forms, or E-mail, depending on what's available.

OPTION #1: A host phones to reschedule a business party with your boss, a Kupperware distributor.

OPTION #2: A person leaves a message for a fellow insurance agent about an automobile accident.

OPTION #3: A coworker's spouse leaves a message about where and when to pick up a child.

OPTION #4: An attorney phones with information on an upcoming court appearance.

Writing Instructions 1

"Signs, signs, everywhere signs. Do this. Don't do that. Can't you read the signs?" Have you heard this song before? Is this what signs are about—people bossing you around?

Instructions are like signs, but they aren't written to be bossy. Instead, they are tools that writers give to readers to make work simple and safe. The blueprints for the building, the sheet music for the song, the pattern for the dress—these are all work instructions.

READ: For a 24-hour period, pay attention to written instructions. Keep a log of each time you come across a sign telling you what to do. (But don't attempt to do this while driving!) For each sign or set of instructions, describe its subject, purpose, and characteristics. Look for these instructions everywhere, from your toothpaste tube to the bus to the classroom and your part-time job. At the end of your log, summarize what you learned about instructions and their place in daily life.

SHARE your summary with two classmates. Can you agree on three reasons why instructions are important? Write your conclusions below.

1.

2.

3.

RESEARCH: Now that you've thought about instructions for daily living, think about instructions in the workplace.

1. Turn to "Writing Instructions" (218-219) in your handbook. Read the guidelines and the sample instructions.

2. Examine closely the "Hand-Washing Procedure" used by hospital staff (on page 160).

REFLECT: Once you have examined these models, reflect on the questions below:

1. What is the general aim of workplace instructions? What is the specific aim of the "hand-washing" model?

2. How do writers make their instructions easy for readers to understand?

3. How do writers sometimes make their instructions difficult to use?

ENRICHMENT: Test out instructions in class. Choose a set of instructions that can be completed in the classroom. Bring any materials listed in the instructions and observe classmates working through the process. Do the instructions make the process easy to complete or not? Explore the reasons why or why not together.

City Hospital of the Immaculate
Orange Grove, California

HAND-WASHING PROCEDURE

Perform this procedure whenever you report for duty and before and after providing care for an infected or contaminated patient. Also use this procedure after personal bathroom use, eating, coughing, or sneezing, and before and after using sterile gloves, gowns, and masks. WHENEVER IN DOUBT, WASH YOUR HANDS!

Steps in the Procedure:

NOTE: Jewelry such as rings harbor bacteria and are difficult to clean. You should not wear jewelry in the hospital workplace. If your hands accidentally touch the inside of the sink or any other article during this procedure, you must start over.

1. Remove the first paper towel, and discard it into the wastebasket.

2. Take the next paper towel and use it to turn the water on to a comfortable temperature. DO NOT TOUCH THE CONTROLS WITH YOUR HANDS.

3. Put your hands and wrists under the running water, keeping your fingertips pointed downward. Allow the water to flow gently.

4. Once your hands and wrists are completely wet, apply antiseptic solution.

5. Bring your hands together and create a heavy lather. Wash at least 3 inches above the wrists, and get soap under your fingernails and between your fingers. WASH WELL FOR ONE FULL MINUTE.

6. With the fingertips of your opposite hand, circle each finger on the other hand with a rotary motion from base to tip. Pay careful attention to the area between your fingers, around nail beds, and under your fingernails.

7. Rinse your hands well under running water. HOLD YOUR HANDS DOWN so that the direction of the water flow is from the wrist to your fingertips.

8. Pat your hands dry with a clean paper towel, and turn off the water with the towel. Discard the paper towel into the wastebasket.

Writing Instructions 2

WRITE: You are now ready to create a set of instructions. Check out in your handbook, one last time, the process of generating instructions (218), and then work through one of the following options. Fit your instructions on one or two pages.

OPTION #1: A school-related activity: Draft a set of instructions for surviving your toughest course, choosing a career, planning the prom, or eating in the cafeteria.

OPTION #2: A home-related task: Examine the chores you do in your home. Choose one or two to explain to the robot you have just purchased to take over these tasks. (Write carefully! Robots will do exactly what you tell them to do.)

OPTION #3: A task you enjoy: Do you write lyrics and compose your own music? Do you have a knack for solving math word problems? Do you write poetry? Can you climb rocks really well? Turn your interest into instructions for amateurs.

OPTION #4: A familiar work task: What processes have you learned in a summer or part-time job? Imagine that you have to leave instructions for a temporary replacement while you take a mini-vacation.

OPTION #5: A class-related process: In one of your classes, are you learning a process that is performed in a particular workplace? Imagine you are in that workplace and draft the instructions for workers who need to know how to do the job.

OPTION #6: A future career task: Are you curious about a process or activity that may be a part of your work in the future? Research that process and write a set of instructions for yourself.

OPTION #7: Researching a career: Are you interested in a specific profession? Research it and then instruct someone else about how to prepare for that career.

OPTION #8: Giving directions: You need to have a fragile parcel of fine china delivered to an address across town. Draft instructions to a delivery person in your organization explaining how to get it there safely.

Other Options:

Are you still undecided? Write instructions for completing one of the following processes:

a. faxing a letter

b. changing a tire

c. purchasing a home computer

d. making a home energy-efficient

e. changing a car's oil

f. planting a garden

g. using a checkbook

h. giving someone a perm

Writing Summaries

Sometimes you have to take time to save time. That's what summaries are all about in today's information-rich workplace. When workers take the time to write effective summaries, they save readers a lot of time—because a good summary gives readers just the essential information they need.

Summaries and Everyday Life

In surprising ways, summaries are part of our daily experience. Think about the following real-life summaries:

- At the beginning of the video you rented are several movie previews.

- At the end of the nightly news, the weatherperson recaps the forecast and a news anchor capsulizes a major story.

- During Monday's study hall, you share stories with friends about what you did on the weekend.

REFLECT: With the examples above in mind, work through the following:

1. List three or four other examples of summaries.

2. Consider all these examples. What do they tell you about the function of summaries?

WRITE: Test your ability to write a clear and accurate summary by doing the following group activity:

1. Watch a TV program (could be a drama, sitcom, or news magazine) or read a magazine article.

2. After watching the program (or reading the article), each group member writes a summary of it.

3. Compare your summaries. Which is most clear and most accurate? Why?

Summaries and the Workplace

Who writes summaries and why? Who reads them and why? Knowing the answers to these questions will help you write effective workplace summaries.

READ: Turn to "Writing Summaries" (220-224) in your handbook. After reading the explanations and models, answer the following questions:

1. What does writing a summary involve?

2. What is the relationship between the original (document, meeting, conference, etc.) and the summary? What are the similarities? What are the differences?

ANALYZE: Summaries help readers be informed and make informed decisions. Workers use summaries for the following reasons:

   (a) to get the main points without having to read or experience the whole
   (b) to decide whether reading or experiencing the whole would be useful
   (c) to get an overview of key points before addressing details

For each of the situations below, explore the usefulness of the summary by matching a letter (or letters) above to it. *Note:* There may be more than one right answer, so be prepared to give reasons.

.... A dietician reads an article summarizing a scientific study on eating fish to prevent cancer.

.... A hotel manager reads a report by her head chef who attended a weeklong seafood preparation workshop.

.... A production supervisor for a furniture manufacturer reads the introduction to a book on the quality-circle concept.

.... A reporter reads a press release from Habitat for Humanity concerning the dedication of one of its homes.

.... A nursing-home nurse reads the discharge summary of a patient just transferred from a hospital.

REACT: The article below is from the *American Institute for Cancer Research Newsletter* (Summer 1995, Issue 48), and it summarizes Dr. John A. Milner's research regarding the use of garlic to suppress cancer. Read the summary and answer these questions:

● Who may want to know whether garlic can suppress cancer (list three occupations)?

● Why may each of these people prefer to read a summary rather than a full report?

● The author quotes Dr. Milner three times. Do the quotations make the summary more interesting? Why?

Garlic May Offer More Than Flavor
Research Shows Cancer-Suppressing Potential

Garlic gives many foods a distinctive, delicious flavor without adding fat—making it a popular choice with health-conscious cooks. This aromatic seasoning is also of considerable interest to researchers for its potential to fight cancer.

Garlic's effects on breast cancer are being explored by John A. Milner, Ph.D., at Penn State University's Department of Nutrition. Supported by a grant from American Institute for Cancer Research, Dr. Milner was among the first to investigate garlic's cancer-preventive potential; now a new AICR grant is helping him find out how garlic may inhibit the development of breast cancer, as well as how other dietary factors may influence garlic's effectiveness.

Dr. Milner's work shows that garlic may suppress tumor development in two ways: by inhibiting the metabolism of carcinogens in the body and by stopping them from binding to the genetic material. In his studies, laboratory rats fed garlic powder had far fewer breast tumors than their counterparts who were not fed garlic powder when both were exposed to cancer-causing agents.

Results of Dr. Milner's research also show that garlic seems to be most effective at preventing cancers in rats fed high-fat diets—particularly diets high in corn oil and other unsaturated fats. "However, this should not be seen as an endorsement of high-fat diets," he cautions. "Garlic seems to have little effectiveness when the diet is high in saturated fat." He adds that excessive amounts of protein in the diet may also suppress garlic's ability to act against carcinogens.

"The results of this study may help explain some of the variability observed between dietary habits and cancer risk," Dr. Milner notes. "Population studies show that people in different parts of the world who consume similar amounts of fat can have very different rates of cancer incidence. Garlic and other elements in the diet may account for some of the difference. However, the whole issue is very complex. We need to get a better handle on it before making dietary recommendations," he adds.

Garlic's benefits may not be limited to just breast cancer—researchers have found garlic to be useful against cancers of the liver, lung, and colon as well. Clinical trials involving human patients are currently underway to determine how much garlic is needed in the diet to achieve cancer protection. "I believe that the amount will probably be quite small," predicts Dr Milner. That's another good reason to keep garlic in mind the next time you're in the kitchen.

Writing Summaries of Documents

Writing a good summary involves making decisions about what's most important in an original document.

CHOOSE: From the list below, *circle* items you should include in a summary and *cross out* those that you would leave out.

conclusions	specific details	recommendations
main points	facts and figures	examples
opinions	explanations	outcomes
purpose	background info	jargon

ANALYZE: When writing a summary, you will save time by highlighting the original text in order to pull out key points. Here are some highlighting tips:

1. Photocopy the document or print an extra copy to mark up.

2. Use a highlighter or colored pen to mark key words and phrases.

3. Pay attention to topic and concluding sentences of paragraphs. They often signal and summarize the paragraph's key point.

4. Look for transitional words that say "Listen up!" These words can

- number.................... first, second, next, finally
- compare, contrast, link .... although, furthermore
- show cause and effect .... because, therefore
- stress importance .... major, crucial, basically

Note: Turn to "Transitions and Linking Words," 114 in your handbook, for more examples.

SUMMARIZE: With these highlighting tips fresh in mind, do the following:

- Read through Burnette Sawyer's speech "Save Now or Pay Later" (431-432) to get the main idea.

- Reread the speech and highlight (on a photocopy) or list the main points.

- Draft a summary of her speech based on these main points.

WRITE: Review your handbook's material on summaries (220-224), especially the guidelines "Summarizing a Document" and the model "Suiting Up for Success" (223). Now draft your own summary:

1. Pick a work-related topic that interests you, and find an article (two to three pages) similar to "Suiting Up for Success."

2. Photocopy the article.

3. Follow the steps for summarizing a document (221). Be sure to highlight your copy. Then list the main points below.

INSIDE

How short or long should a summary be? Good question. The answer is this: as long as it needs to be. That is, the length of your summary should be determined by how you see your reader using it:

1. to get a brief description of the document?
2. to get the main facts?
3. to get a deeper understanding of the issue?

The more your reader needs, the longer your summary should be.

Writing Short Reports

How did you feel about your last report card? Whether it gave you pleasure or pain, it's a practical piece of workplace writing—a short report evaluating your strengths, weaknesses, and progress. Short reports—like your report card—share information for a practical purpose.

READ & REACT: Turn to "Workplace Writing Tasks" (183) in your handbook. Study the "Reports, Memos" section of the table and answer the following questions:

1. What do you think these reports have in common?

2. What kinds of information would be found in these reports?

3. What purpose might these reports serve in an organization?

DEFINE: Read "Writing Short Reports," (227) in your handbook, and imagine that you're Dan Altena, the deputy sheriff quoted at the top of the page. Then imagine that you're writing a report on a car accident in which someone was seriously injured. Choose two guidelines under "Preparing the Report" and explain why each would help you do your job well.

1.

2.

ANALYZE: Carefully read Eric Rowe's AWOL report in your handbook (228-229). Analyze this short report by answering these questions:

1. Who is the report's reader? How is the report designed with this reader in mind?

2. What is the purpose of the report? To **(a)** inform; **(b)** inform and analyze; or **(c)** inform, analyze, and persuade? Make a copy of the report and highlight sections that perform these different functions.

3. What information is presented in the report? Is it understandable? Does it appear to be factual and accurate? How can you tell?

FOLLOW UP: Practice your reporting skills by drafting a short report for your classmates on your experience of one of the following:

- fashion trends
- CD's or books you have purchased
- a place you have visited recently
- your favorite sports team's season (finished or in progress)
- a part-time job, internship, or summer job
- something impressive you've learned recently

On-the-Job Report

In any situation, mistakes do happen. When one happens on the job, the error must be corrected, and often reports must be filed to explain what happened and what needs to be done to correct it.

COMPLETE the "Spoilage and Make-Over Report" on the next page using the details below:

PROBLEM:

On February 16, 1995, Spencer Farmany discovered in his proofreading department that an error was made in the production of 500 copies of Job Number 41990 for the Mundi Book Company. Unfortunately, neither Stephanie Rumsey in the typesetting department nor Tim Langsford in Print Shop No. 4 read the work order carefully. The book was ordered to be set in the newer Optima typestyle but instead was run in the Schoolbook typestyle. The book must be completely redone.

SOLUTION:

To change the computer files to the correct type font and output new film, it will take two people in the production department 6 hours each. Then it will require Tim 10 more hours to print the 100-page books. They are being printed 4 pages per sheet of paper; the sheets cost 10 cents each. Each cover costs 20 cents. Each of the three workers is paid $8 an hour.

Hint: The chart below may help you calculate more accurately so that your figures on the report are clear and correct.

Production Costs			Printing Costs			Paper/Cover Costs		
Number Hours	Wage/ Hour	Total Cost	Number Hours	Wage/ Hour	Total Cost	Number Sheets	Cost/ Sheet	Total Cost

COMPLETE: For many standard reports, workers complete specially designed forms. Complete the "Spoilage and Make-Over Report" below using the details from page 169.

SPOILAGE AND MAKE-OVER REPORT

CUSTOMER ....

JOB NO. .... **DATE** ....

ERROR NOTED BY ....

REASON FOR MAKE-OVER ....

....

....

....

....

DEPT. RESPONSIBLE FOR ERROR ....

**THE FOLLOWING IS NEEDED
TO MAKE CORRECTION** ....

....

....

....

MATERIAL SPOILED				LABOR/TIME LOST				
QTY.	DESCRIPTION	UNIT COST	TOTAL COST	HRS.	DEPT.	NO. OF PERSONS	UNIT COST	TOTAL COST
	Total Material					Total Labor		

The Career Report

WRITE: Work on your reporting skills by developing a short report for one of the following options. Take another look at "Writing Short Reports" (227-229), think carefully about the information you need, and consider your organizational options.

OPTION #1: Interview three of your classmates about their career plans and write a report. (Check out "Conducting Interviews," 341-344 in your handbook.)

OPTION #2: Shadow someone in a career you find interesting, and write an AWOL report similar to Eric Rowe's (228-229 in your handbook).

OPTION #3: Keep a log of the work you do for one week during an internship, volunteer work, or a part-time job. At the end of the week, write a work report on your activities.

OPTION #4: Think about your course work and career plans. Is there a specific report you could write based on that work? For example, if you are an auto technician student, you could write a vehicle inspection report. If you are a design student, you could write a report on the latest software available for design work.

Writing Workshops

Searching and Selecting

Taking Stock of Your Writing

Here is a chance for you to take stock of your writing experiences and abilities at the beginning of the year. This information will make it easier for you to evaluate your writing progress later in the year when you refer back to this survey.

1. What are the last pieces of writing you have completed? (Identify two or three.)

2. What forms of writing are you most familiar with? (Reports, essays, paragraphs, memos, reviews, stories, poems, essay-test answers, etc.)

3. What is the most successful or meaningful paper you've written in the past year or two? Briefly describe it.

4. Do you usually write on subjects of your own choosing or on assigned topics? Which do you like better and why?

5. What is your greatest strength as a writer? Explain.

6. What stage in the writing process gives you the most trouble? (Getting started, focusing your efforts, organizing, drafting, revising, editing?) Explain.

7. Do you follow a set revising strategy? What sorts of changes do you normally make when you revise?

8. What type of writing gives you the most problems? What type of writing would you like to learn more about? What specific writing skills do you need to practice?

INSIDE

info

Read "The Writing Process" in your handbook (004). As you read, decide how your own process of writing matches up with the one in the handbook. Do you follow most or all of the same steps?

Systems Check

READ: Read about the writing process in the handbook (001-009). As you read, decide how well your own process of writing matches up with this discussion. Have you found the points made in the handbook to be true for you? Are there points you disagree with? Are there any points missing?

REACT: Note below at least two specific things you have learned over the past few years (months, days) about your personal process of writing. (Maybe you've learned that writing never gets any easier for you, or you've established an effective revising technique, or . . .)

1. ....

....

2. ....

....

3. ....

....

REVIEW: Look through the rest of "The Writing Process" section (010-057). Note three lists, guidelines, sections, etc., that you feel will be helpful as you work to improve your skills as a writer. (Provide the heading and topic number for each.)

1. ....

....

2. ....

....

3. ....

....

follow-up Share the results of all of your reading, reacting, and reviewing with a classmate or writing group. Learn as much as you can about writing from each other's experiences and insights.

Pro or Con

READ & REACT: Let's suppose you've been asked to write an essay of argumentation—that is, an essay in which you argue for or against a point of view concerning a timely issue. How might you go about planning a strategy for selecting a subject? In the space below, list four references to the handbook (lists, guidelines, sections, etc.) that would help you in your search.

1. ....

....

2. ....

....

3. ....

....

4. ....

....

SELECT: Put your selecting strategy into action by working through the handbook references in the order you have listed them until you identify two good writing ideas for an essay of argumentation. List your choices below. (Use your own paper to complete any selecting activities like free writing or clustering.)

EXTEND: Write freely for 10 minutes about one of these two subjects. Afterward, note any ideas in your writing that present solid arguments in favor of your point of view. (Share your work.) Then continue working on your essay and make your argument even better.

INSIDE

Write from experience, from a need to know, from a genuine interest in a subject. Doing otherwise makes about as much sense as trying out for the school chorus even though you have no interest in singing.

Talk to Yourself

"Writing is easy," said the well-known sportswriter Red Smith. "All you have to do is sit down at a typewriter and open a vein."

Right now, let's assume that you have been asked to "open a vein." Maybe your teacher has said, "You'll have 10 minutes for free writing." Free writing is also known as **impromptu writing**, **writing bursts**, or **stop 'n' write**.

Whatever the name, the problem is the same: how to get started, go hard, and bring your writing in for a landing without crashing and burning (getting writer's block). Nobody can give you strict rules for what is supposed to be a free and creative process. But you can learn to write better at high speed *if* you will learn how to talk to yourself as you write.

LISTEN: For this exercise you don't need to mumble or move your lips. Instead, activate the quiet voice inside your head that whispers encouragement to you as you're going along, a voice that improves your attitude, increases your energy, raises your ambition, and broadens your interest. Listen to some of the words a writer's brain might whisper:

get going

try it

faster, faster

use shorthand

what's it all about?

let go of yourself

what else?

aha!   what's the difference?

what comes next?

so what?

prove it

don't erase   show it

why?

how do I feel?

do some more

what do I think?

follow-up Now, start writing about a general topic of your own choosing. Let your inner voice drive you on. *Never* talk back to it!

Generating Texts

Setting Limits

The process of choosing and limiting a writing subject is a series of logical steps. First you think, "I'd like to write something about . . . popular music." Then you have to get more specific—say, popular music during the Vietnam War. Then a bit more specific. How about the war songs of a specific artist (or group)? Perhaps you want to go a step further and focus on one or two of the artist's songs. Now that's a subject you could deal with fairly effectively in a few pages. That's what we mean by limiting a subject.

REACT: Okay, your subject is TV commercials. Your mission, to narrow and shape this broad subject into a topic that you could write about effectively in a one-page report. Use the space below to begin narrowing your subject. As a guide, refer to the "Guidelines for Searching and Shaping a Subject" in your handbook (015-016).

EXTEND: Either make a list of ideas that you would include in your writing about the narrowed topic, or freely write a first draft to see what you can discover. (Share your results.)

INSIDE

info

When you're not sure whether your subject is limited or specific enough for an assignment, make an outline (or list) of related facts and details. If the outline goes on and on to include all kinds of information, then chances are you have to go back and narrow your subject further.

Imaginary Dialogues

As a writer, I often hold imaginary conversations in my head. I do this whenever I need to talk about something, particularly if it's exciting or upsetting. It helps me handle real conversations when they come along.

You can use an imaginary dialogue to explore a writing subject. The two speakers can be real or imaginary, but they should each have a different point of view. And they should each be motormouths so that they reveal as much as possible about the subject.

CONVERSE: Look at the following statements and choose the one that you think is the most thought provoking. Using the statement as a starter, create an imaginary dialogue between any two speakers, real or imagined. Choose from the list of possible speakers beneath each statement.

● **Statement:**   High-school boys and girls are equally concerned about their looks.

Speakers: Two high-school boys
Two high-school girls
Parents of high-school students

● **Statement:**   The customer is always right.

Speakers: The business owner and a manager
Two coworkers
Two customers

● **Statement:**   The United States is ready for a woman president.

Speakers: Two men
Two women
A man and a woman

follow-up   Read the dialogue you have created and underline the ideas, details, and phrases that give you a better feel for the subject. Write a brief paragraph expanding on what you have underlined.

Ask the Write Questions

After you've chosen a writing subject, but before you begin writing a first draft, you must shape your subject somehow. Shaping a writing subject can include narrowing it down if it's too broad, gathering details, and getting a well-rounded feel for the subject and all of its aspects.

Say you have to write an essay of definition in which you define the term "ambition." For this workshop, use the section in your handbook called "Guidelines for Searching and Shaping a Subject" to work your subject into shape for writing (015-016).

REVIEW: Review what your handbook says about using "Structured Questions" to shape your subject.

APPLY: Apply three or more structured questions to the topic of "ambition." Ask yourself the questions and answer them as completely and thoughtfully as you can. Try to include one structured question of your own. Use your own paper to record your answers.

REFLECT: Compare the information you and one of your classmates managed to gather using the structured questions. Discuss your initial reactions to this shaping strategy.

---

follow-up Answer a few more structured questions if you want to gather more
→ information. Then write a first draft for an essay defining "ambition."

First or Last

There are two distinct ways to arrange the details in your writing: *inductively* and *deductively*. Watch how two different kinds of paragraphs can be developed out of the same sentence. Here's the sentence that will serve as the main idea for each paragraph:

The winter of 1990-91 will be remembered as a costly one.

The first type of paragraph will be arranged inductively. In other words, the statements begin with specific details that eventually guide the reader toward the main idea.

Arctic air masses dipped repeatedly across the nation's midsection. The results were reported on the nightly news. In the Texas panhandle, pipes burst as cloudless skies brought a rare hard freeze. In Tennessee, some 200 cars piled up in a dense fog, and many lives were lost. Many were injured and one was killed in New York City as a short circuit caused by melting snow led to an underground train derailment. In California, old-timers couldn't remember a colder spell than the one that this year ruined nearly 85 percent of the citrus crop, most of the avocados, the strawberries, and the broccoli. The winter of 1990-91 will be remembered as a costly one.

The second type of paragraph is arranged deductively. In other words, the main idea comes first, followed by specific details that serve as illustrations, proofs, or explanations.

The winter of 1990-91 will be remembered as a costly one. As arctic air masses dipped repeatedly across the nation's midsection, the sad results were reported on the nightly news. In the Texas panhandle, pipes burst as cloudless skies brought a rare hard freeze. In Tennessee, some 200 cars piled up in a dense fog, and many lives were lost. Many were injured and one was killed in New York City as a short circuit caused by melting snow led to an underground train derailment. In California, old-timers couldn't remember a colder spell than the one that this year ruined nearly 85 percent of the citrus crop, most of the avocados, the strawberries, and the broccoli.

WRITE: Write a paragraph about some conflict at your school, at your job, or in your community. Decide whether inductive or deductive organization is called for, and use that method consistently.

follow-up Find an article in a newspaper or magazine that is clearly inductive or deductive. Bring it in for a class discussion. Be able to point out the features of the article that make it inductive or deductive.

Chain-Link Sense

The traditional five-paragraph essay that students are asked to write follows a common-sense pattern. But it often leads to writing without passion or good logical development.

Your writing can take on a better organization if you think of the logical *moves* needed, rather than simply the number of paragraphs required. For example, you could use a "cause and effect" pattern of development:

> Miss Goldilocks didn't just "happen" to break into the home of the three bears. IN FACT, she had a number of reasons, a few of which she herself understood only later when she had stopped running. INITIALLY, she was unhappy, in an unfocused sort of way, with her home life. THOUGH SHE HAD NEVER COMPLAINED TO MR. AND MRS. GOLDILOCKS, she unconsciously resented the fact that she was an only child. FURTHERMORE, . . .

Psst! Notice the transitional words (in caps) that signal your logical moves to the reader.

READ: Here are a few of the basic logical patterns you could use, along with the transitional words that could signal your basic moves. Look them over carefully, but remember, you don't have to stick with simple patterns. You can combine them in an infinite variety of sequences. (See 114 in your handbook for a list of useful transitions.)

Some Basic Logical Patterns

Cause and Effect

Move from backgrounds and conditions to outcomes and results. Or start with effects and then back up to show causes. Sometimes many causes lead to one effect. Sometimes many effects spring from one main cause.
Useful transitions:
> *Since . . . initially . . . first . . . in order to . . . because . . . therefore . . . as a result . . . eventually . . . hence . . . so . . . consequently . . .*

Enumeration

Break down a whole into a number of parts. Number the parts and describe them. Give examples if that helps. Single out some for a closer look. Summarize your results.
Useful transitions:
> *First . . . second . . . third . . . finally . . . initially . . . then . . . further . . . moreover . . . one . . . another . . . still another . . . not only . . . but also . . . and . . . for example . . .*

Closer and Closer Examination

See the big picture first. Then move in for a close-up. Finally move in for even finer detail.
Useful transitions:

> *In general . . . overall . . . in particular . . . in fact . . . part of . . . inside the . . . alongside . . . within . . . even . . .*

Wider and Wider Look

Gradually back up from your topic, the way a movie camera does, to show wider implications, a larger context, etc.
Useful transitions:

> *The surrounding . . . even more . . . beyond . . . extending to . . . furthermore . . . all told . . . including . . . the whole . . .*

Comparison and Contrast

Show similarities or differences between two things that belong to the same general family.
Useful transitions:

> *As . . . like . . . unlike . . . comparably . . . on the other hand . . . the opposite . . . similarly . . . whereas . . . just as . . . although . . . both . . . the same is true of . . . more . . . less . . . yet . . .*

Norm and Exceptions

Show what is normal or customary or ordinary. Then explore exceptions to the rule. Explain why they are exceptions. Give examples and explanations.
Useful transitions:

> *Mainly . . . typically . . . the usual . . . normally . . . customarily . . . however . . . yet . . . in some cases . . . though . . . with the exception of . . .*

Logical Conditions

Show the logical sequence that leads from certain premises to certain conclusions.
Useful transitions:

> *If . . . then . . . provided that . . . assuming that . . . supposing . . . despite . . . nevertheless . . . yet . . . whereas . . . consequently . . .*

WRITE: Use one of these logical patterns as the main organizing scheme for a paragraph in which you explain what you hope to be doing with your life 10 years from now.

Take a Stand

Mitchell Ivers, in his excellent book *The Random House Guide to Good Writing*, identifies a six-step process that, if applied and practiced, will turn uncertain writers into confident and persuasive essayists.

REACT: Put Mr. Ivers' process into action by completing the following plan. Do your work on your own paper. (Share your work upon completion.)

1. Choose a subject about which you have a strong opinion. (See 011-013 in your handbook.)

2. Write a focus or thesis statement, identifying what you would like to explain or prove about the subject. (Generally speaking, a dominant feeling or attitude about the subject is expressed in the thesis statement. For help see 018-019 in your handbook.)

3. Identify at least one important counterargument to your thesis. (That is, admit to a possible weakness in your way of thinking, or point out that there is another way to look at your subject.)

4. List five or six points in support of your thesis. (If you can't think of five or six, list as many as you can.)

5. Identify your most persuasive argument or point. (Put a star next to the strongest point you have listed in #4.)

6. Come to some conclusion about your argument. (Decide what it is you have proved or determined through your planning.)

WRITE: The next step is to put your plan into action by writing a first draft of your essay. Develop your writing freely, starting with your thesis statement and then incorporating other ideas from your plan. *A suggestion:* Deal with the counterargument early on, and save your most persuasive argument for the knockout punch near the end of your essay.

Developing Texts

Show, Don't Tell

If your writing just hangs there, lifeless, maybe that's because you're telling too much and showing too little. Lively writing moves the way a hummingbird moves: it darts in to suck up the sweet details and then backs up to look things over. If you spend all of your time looking things over, you and your reader will go hungry. (See "Showing Versus Telling" in your handbook, 063, for two examples of the way showing can give life to bland *telling* statements.)

READ: Here's a telling statement that may sound fairly interesting as it stands:

Roy's mother and father tended his knife wound in a way that showed how deeply they were suffering.

However, this sentence simply tells the reader what to think rather than leading the reader through the thought by showing details. Here is how the acclaimed African-American writer James Baldwin *shows* the idea in *Go Tell It on the Mountain*:

(To fully appreciate this paragraph, listen to it read out loud, and read it out loud yourself.)

His father and mother, a small basin of water between them, knelt by the sofa where Roy lay, and his father was washing the blood from Roy's forehead. It seemed that his mother, whose touch was so much more gentle, had been thrust aside by his father, who could not bear to have anyone else touch his wounded son. And now she watched, one hand in the water, the other in a kind of anguish, at her waist. . . . Her face, as she watched, was full of pain and fear, of tension basely supported, and of pity that could scarcely have been expressed had she filled all the world with her weeping. His father muttered sweet, delirious things to Roy, and his hands, when he dipped them again in the basin and wrung out the cloth, were trembling.

REFLECT: How do you "show" in writing? Think in terms of the 5 W's and H (who, what, when, where, why, and how). Make sure that your writing answers these questions. Also think in terms of the three different types of details: sensory, memory, and reflective. Refer to "Types of Details" in your handbook for more (110).

WRITE: Here are three sentences that tell rather than show. Raise at least one of them from the dead in a "showing" paragraph full of detail. (If none of these sentences suit you, think up your own telling sentence.) Share your results.

1. I had never seen anything like it before.

2. It was a thoughtless thing to do.

3. I could tell my teacher (coach, friend, boss, coworker, etc.) was getting mad.

Right from the Source

If you state an important idea in writing, your readers will know what you think. But if you back up your statement with solid facts and figures, your readers may also begin to believe that what you think is true.

For that reason, experienced writers stay alert for provable facts, quotations, and anecdotes, details that they can use to support their ideas.

READ: Here are some quotations, anecdotes, provable facts, and details that a writer might store away in his or her memory, hoping someday to use them in writing:

Quotations:

1. "The danger of the past was that people became slaves. The danger of the future is that people may become robots." (Erich Gromn)
2. "Leadership is action, not position." (Donald H. McGannon)

Anecdotes:

1. When asked why he wanted to become president, John F. Kennedy replied, "Because that's where the power is!"
2. A certain professor was married to the Countess of Malta. They celebrated their honeymoon aboard the *Andrea Doria*, which had the great misfortune to sink midway through their celebration. He always kept a model of the ship on his desk. When asked why, he would reply, "To remind me that each day could be my last."

Provable Facts and Details:

1. South African black nationalist Nelson R. Mandela was released from prison in 1990, after spending almost 28 years behind bars.
2. Ten of the 13 books that sold more than a million copies during the 1980's were written by only three authors: political-thriller writer Tom Clancy, horror writer Stephen King, and romance novelist Danielle Steele.

REFLECT: In your writing, which should come first, your thoughts or the support you borrow from an authority? Use common sense: If your ideas spring from the words of an authority, place the borrowed material first and follow with your commentary. If you borrow material to support an idea of your own, place your idea first.

WRITE: Practice incorporating borrowed material into your writing. Write a short paragraph that uses one of the items above to reinforce something you have to say.

INSIDE info

Offering plenty of support for your ideas is desirable. However, if you supply too much support and not enough personal commentary, your own voice may be drowned out. Remember that support must support *something*, and that something is your own line of thought.

Branch Out

The next time you try to write a paragraph, take a hint from a tree. Notice how a tree trunk splits into limbs, each limb splits into branches, those split into twigs, and so on.

Writing works like that if you focus on an idea and write away. A topic leads to concepts, each concept leads to two or three ideas, and each of these leads to details. To help you see the details in two branches of thought, writers often hold both branches side by side with a technique called parallel structure. (See 101 and 440 in your handbook.)

READ the paragraph below in which Verne Meyer thinks about how he chose his career.

Work. Get to work! Do your work! I hate to work! Do all people hate to work? What if you liked your work? I mean, really liked it? As a tenth-grade kid on a Minnesota farm, that thought hit me while doing my evening chores—feeding chickens. I hated chickens. I hated their cluck-cluck, cackle-cackle when I walked through a crowd with a grain scoop of feed. I hated their pecking and scratching when I reached my bare fingers under their feathered bottoms to gather eggs. I hated angry hens erupting out of nests and into my face. I hated work. But I liked play. I liked reading books by Jack London, Mark Twain, and Willa Cather. I liked packing a head full of thought and a heart full of feeling into one thin poem. I liked acting out plays, building sets, rigging lights, and making beards out of crepe hair and spirit gum. So that afternoon, leaning on my grain scoop in a crowd of cackling egg-layers, I chose a career in which I could do what I liked. I decided to become an English teacher.

REFLECT: Notice how the opening, one-word sentence leads to three parallel sentences, and how those lead to three more. Notice how the long sentence about being a "tenth-grade kid" introduces "chickens," and that word leads to a series of sentences about chickens. All together, the first 13 sentences describe one branch of thought that Meyer labels "work." Then he looks down another branch that he calls "play." To help us see how both concepts are part of the same topic (his career search), Meyer puts "play" and "work" side by side in one paragraph.

Psst! It won't take you long to figure out that the "twins" in paragraphs like these are more like "fraternal" twins than "identical" ones. In other words, you won't find many perfect parallels. Writers give enough parallel structure so that we can notice the parallel, but not so much that we feel we're watching a boring mechanical device like a teeter-totter or a pendulum.

WRITE: Pull together your thoughts about activities that you like or dislike. Then write away, following topics until they split into concepts, ideas, and details. After you've put all your thoughts on paper, cut, rearrange, and refine until your writing is clear.

Good Backup

Anyone can make a confident-sounding statement. For example, in a review of *Raiders of the Lost Ark*, you might say:

It's the movie Hollywood was born to make.

But conscientious writers back up their statements with evidence to show that what they say is true, like this:

The author lists details to explain why the film is particularly suited to Hollywood, or why Hollywood was born to make it.

The author gives background details to support the opening statement.

It's the movie Hollywood was born to make, and was born making. It has buried treasures and Nazi villains, poison darts and mystical wraiths, damsels in distress and Arabian swordsmen, snake pits, submarines, booby-trapped jungle caverns, Himalayan taverns, Egyptian bazaars, and an archeologist hero with the grit of Bogart, the dash of Gable, and the fearlessness of Superman. It's a movie that harks back to the cliff-hanging thrills of *The Perils of Pauline*, that reinvents the Saturday-matinee serials of the 1930's and 1940's with an edge-of-the-seat style that will hypnotize kids and reawaken in adults their primal memories of what moviegoing was once all about. It's called *Raiders of the Lost Ark*, and it's about as pure an example of the Hollywood summer movie as anything since *Jaws* and *Star Wars*.

REACT: In this *Newsweek* review, David Ansen gives evidence to support his statements. Expand the following statements by adding two sentences containing evidence for each premise.

A. You need to be especially alert when driving on the freeway.

1. ....

....

2. ....

....

B. Being a good student is not an easy job.

1. ....

....

2. ....

....

Building an Argument

Let's talk about a specific point in the process of building an argument. When reading, researching, and thinking to prepare an argument, be sure to ask this question: What objections to my position can I expect? If you can anticipate these objections, you can plan how to deal with them (concede them) in your writing. Making concessions will not weaken your position if it is based on solid thinking. In fact, conceding tends to strengthen an argument by taking away the opposition's scoring potential.

READ & REACT: Below are statements of opinion that, when supported by facts, are the backbone of an argument. Read and react to them with a classmate. Do you agree with the statements? Why or why not? After you've thought about each one for a few minutes, write at least one solid objection in the space provided. Make sure each of your objections is thoughtful and reasonable. (Not "Well, what do you know?")

Part-time, minimum-wage jobs are worthwhile for high-school students because students gain valuable workplace experiences.

Objection: ....

....

....

....

While adults are responsible for offering an education that can lead to career opportunities, high-school students are responsible for getting the education and seeking the opportunities.

Objection: ....

....

....

....

The music industry should voluntarily rate albums, just as movies are rated, so that customers know which albums contain obscenity or adult themes.

Objection: ....

....

....

....

....

APPLY: With your partner, build a brief argument (a paragraph) based on one of the statements of opinion and related objection from above. Use the following patterns as a guide for making any concessions. (Share your results.)

- It is true that . . . However . . . Therefore . . .
- Of course . . . But . . . So . . .
- I admit that . . . On the other hand . . . In short . . .

INSIDE

The main argument, or statement of opinion, is called the *central claim* in the arguing biz. To learn more about building arguments, refer to your handbook (559-574).

Extending Metaphors

Do you remember what a metaphor is? According to your handbook, it's a figure of speech comparing two unlike things in which no words of comparison (*like* or *as*) are used. For example: *The sprinkler raised its peacock tail in the backyard.* (See 486 in your handbook for a list of other figures of speech.)

Sometimes a good metaphor will suggest a whole series of similarities between your writing idea and the thing you are comparing it to. You might s-t-r-e-t-c-h a metaphor like that to fill a paragraph or more. This stretched metaphor is known as an **extended metaphor**.

An extended metaphor can describe a scene, an event, a character, or an emotion in a new and powerful way. *Psst!* Stretching or extending a metaphor works best for a special effect. Don't overuse this technique or your writing will sound artificial and forced.

READ: Carefully read the following paragraph containing a central metaphor that has been turned into an extended metaphor. Underline the central metaphor and pay special attention to the words and phrases that extend it.

My supervisor's garden center was a symphony of color, and she was the conductor. Price gun in hand, she would step confidently to the rose bushes and spread her hands before them. With a quick downbeat her prices slipped between the sharp thorns. Shaking her head emphatically, she seemed driven by the floral music that only she heard. Row after row, finally, exhausted, my supervisor bowed her head, admired her triumphant repricing performance, and turned slowly toward the evergreens.

follow-up Write a short paragraph about another person, comparing his or her actions to those of a painter, boxer, ball player, dancer, clown, . . . in an extended metaphor.

Transformations

After a caterpillar has slept for a while in its cocoon, it is transformed into a butterfly. Transformations occur in writing, too, when a writer takes the substance from one piece of writing and recasts it in a new form. You can use transformations to develop new drafts of your work, especially in the early stages of exploring.   Read on to learn how these transformations work.

READ: Here are some short transformations to serve as illustrations. Start with a "base text" like this paragraph from a student's first draft:

When I was little I had a great interest in drawing. Unfortunately, as I grew older, I neglected this talent, so I was very pleased when I came across piles of my artwork. By looking at these drawings, I was able to recall immediately what other interests I had when I was younger.

Transformation 1: List

Forgotten childhood interests—dinosaurs—airplanes—spaceships—horses—imaginary beasts

Transformation 2: Sentence Fragments

Came across my old artwork. Lots of drawings. In the attic. Took me back. Showed me myself. My interests. Crayoned rockets. Penciled dinosaurs. Poster-painted airplanes and fantastic beasts. Forgot about all that.

Transformation 3: Prepositional Phrases

In the attic. In a box. On paper. With crayon, poster paints, pencil, and construction paper. From the imagination. By me. After many years. Like a time machine.

Transformation 4: Poetry

I took the lid off my childhood
and there, in paint, pencil, and passion
were my long-lost dinosaurs,
the planes my dreams flew,
and the horses of many stripes.

REFLECT: Each one of these transformations brings out something new. The list brings out the contents of the pictures. The fragments sound like a mind thinking. The prepositional phrases lead to the concept of a time machine, and the poetry recaptures some of the feelings of childhood. Each offers a new slant on the topic.

WRITE: Choose a short piece of your own writing, something that you would like to develop further. Write as many different transformations of it as time and interest permit. In addition to the four types already mentioned, here are other transformations to consider. Make up others of your own.

- Describe only sounds.

- Write in exclamations!

- Write it as a memo.

- Turn it into questions.

- Write it as a dialogue or play script.

- Write it as a job description.

Audience Appeal

If you were talking on a telephone and knew that the FBI was listening on a wiretap, wouldn't that affect what you said? If you were giving a speech at your school and found out that the president of the United States was going to be in the audience that day, wouldn't you choose your words carefully?

Now consider your writing. Who is your audience? And how does your definition of that audience affect what you will write? In writing, you define your audience in several ways:

- by choosing a **topic** of interest to certain readers,

- by writing in a certain **style** so that in it your readers will see reflections of themselves,

- by choosing **where to publish** or share your work,

- and sometimes by **directly addressing** readers and telling them how to respond.

In the end, everything hinges on your awareness of the interests, needs, wants, and sensitivities of the readers you want to reach.

READ: Here is a portion of a rap lyric written by Lisa Frederick that first appeared in *New Youth Connections: The Magazine Written By and For New York Youth.* Read it, appreciate it, and think about the audience for whom it was written.

Tell Him Why

Excuse me, do I know you? Do you know me?

Yes, I do know you. You're the brother hanging on the corner with nothing to do

Now you have nerve telling me about myself
When you have empty pockets on the right and emptier pockets on the left

Just because I ignore your hisses, ain't no need for disses
I'll treat you like a mister if you treat me like a missus

I'm telling you this 'cause I'm sick and tired
There's a difference between being heckled and being admired

It's lewd, it's crude, it's downright rude

But in your head you're thinking, "What the heck"
And when a sista walks by you give her no respect

I'm a young female and I'm black too
And in this day and age, that's two strikes against you

So don't give me no stress because you fail to impress
If my own people give me nothing, others will give me still less

Imagine that you are an employee who was treated by another employee in an offensive manner similar to the experience in the rap poem. Write a memo (215 in your handbook) to the other person, or write a letter of complaint (197-198) to the employer. Make up necessary details like the name of the company, the person involved, behavior of the other person, etc.

Reviewing Texts

Feeling Your OAQS

Here's a simple and effective four-step scheme you can use to comment on early drafts in peer-editing sessions:

Observe
Appreciate
Question
Suggest

- **Observe** means to notice what another person's writing is designed to do and then to say something about that design, or purpose. *For example*, you might say, "Even though you are writing about your coworkers, it appears that you are trying to get a message across to your supervisor."

- **Appreciate** means to praise something in the writing that impresses or pleases you. You can find something to appreciate in any piece of writing. *For example*, you might say, "With your description, I can actually see the lightning-damaged computer."

- **Question** means to ask whatever you truly want to know after you've read the piece of writing. You might ask for background information, or a definition, or an explanation. *For example*, you might say, "Why didn't you tell us what happened after the meeting?"

- **Suggest** means to give thoughtful advice about anything you think might help the writing "be all that it can be." Don't expect the other person to take your advice. Just offer it, honestly and courteously. Be specific, and be positive. *For example*, you might say, "With a little more physical detail—especially sound and smell—your third paragraph could be the focus of your writing. What do you think?"

READ: How would you respond to the following piece? It's the first paragraph of an essay exactly as it was written by a student:

> Remembering back to when I was just a little girl, I think of the innocence that has been lost in a pool of anger and mistakes. So many things that meant so much when I was younger were the things that I so freely gave away in moments of rebellion and confusion. Each transition in my life led me further and further away from those times when decisions were so simple. Nothing had to do with values or beliefs. Life was as easy as what pleased Momma and Daddy the most. Just elementary conditions.

Psst! Don't assume that this paragraph is perfect. It's not. And don't assume that the writer knows how to improve it, or that even if she knew how to improve it, she would want to. You'll have to use tact so that she won't feel threatened.

WRITE: Use the space provided here to make tactful comments to the author of the previous paragraph. Use the four-step approach:

O ....
....
....
....

A ....
....
....
....

Q ....
....
....
....

S ....
....
....
....

follow-up → When you've made your own comments, exchange them with two or more others and compare your responses. Learn from each other. Then discuss with your partners what the very best response to this paragraph would be. By now, you should be "feeling your OAQS."

Think About It

If you've developed a draft and are ready to revise it, put on the brakes for a while. Remember, fools rush in where editors fear to tread.

Before you edit for spelling and grammatical correctness, you have bigger matters to attend to. Above all, you need to think about the ideas you have expressed.

Have you kept to your topic? Have you found a worthwhile focus? Have you introduced one or more main ideas? Have you supported your ideas with convincing evidence and helpful explanations? Have you avoided sloppy logic and unwarranted opinions? Have you reached a sensible conclusion?

READ & REACT: Evaluate the quality of thought in the following paragraph of student writing. Don't worry about the writing style; rather, concentrate on the ideas presented. Write your observations in the space below.

> Winning the lottery must be everyone's number one dream! If I won the lottery, my life would be wonderful. First, I'd travel to other countries. I've always wanted to go to Italy and eat spaghetti in a gondola. Then I'd buy an old fastback Mustang with a stardust paint job. My dad says that old Fords aren't mechanically sound. But he's just an old fuddy-duddy. Everyone knows Mustangs are totally hot-looking cars. I'd buy my mom a new car too. She'd probably want a Volvo or something dull like that, but I'd talk her into a Jeep. Some 4x4 action would spice up her life. Yeah, I'm going to keep buying those lottery tickets. A million-dollar prize is definitely worth a buck.

REFLECT: What assumptions does the writer make about other people? What are the bases for her assumptions? What conclusions does she draw? Do the facts she offers support her conclusions? What would you do to improve the quality of thought in this paragraph? Write your observations in the space below. (Share your results.)

....

....

....

....

....

....

How Does It Measure Up?

Suppose a member of your writing group gave you a paragraph and asked you to review it. What would you say? What would you focus on?

Here are some suggestions: When you review a piece of writing, start with a fair attitude, ready to notice both the good and the bad. Focus on the writing, not the writer. Be ready to pay close attention to everything about the writing, large features and small. And finally, organize your thinking by using a good set of criteria.

READ: Study the paragraph below. Then read the set of statements on the next page; use these as a "measuring stick" for the quality of this paragraph. After you've read the criteria, reread the paragraph in light of them.

Driving Me Crazy

If there is one thing that really drives me crazy, it is getting stuck behind a car that is going way under the speed limit. And, naturally, this always seems to happen when I'm already well on my way to being late. A feeling of anxiety mixed with aggravation soon begins to surface in me as I wait impatiently for the solid yellow line to turn to dashes. When it does, I am frustrated further to find that cars are again coming from the other direction, and I must wait longer still. Finally comes the time when I'm free to pass. I switch on my blinker and start to accelerate into the other lane. But wait! The other car, which I am now alongside of, accelerates, not allowing me to pass. I look ahead to see that a car is now coming from the other direction, and I must slow down and get back into my lane. My aggravation turns to anger as the Sunday driver, still ahead of me, again slows down, and I'm right back where I started.

REACT: Here is a series of basic statements about a piece of writing. Place a check mark in the proper blank space to show if you mostly agree (+) or mostly disagree (-) with each statement you apply to "Driving Me Crazy." Afterward, write in your comment to explain how you arrived at your judgment.

Psst! It's one thing to have good criteria, but you also have to set high standards for using the criteria. Think of a grocer with an expensive scale—she or he still has to keep the scale in good condition and read it accurately. When you apply the criteria to "Driving Me Crazy," will you consistently demand the most and the best from it, or will you take a lazy, all-accepting attitude?

+	−	**Criteria**	**Your Own Comments**
....	....	The paragraph is fully developed.	
....	....	The paragraph is well focused.	
....	....	It has a clear purpose.	
....	....	It is sure to please its intended audience.	

HANDBOOK HELPER: In your handbook you can find a different set of criteria for evaluating a piece of writing. Refer to the list of "Traits of an Effective Style" (059). The traits include concreteness, focus, vitality, originality, grace, and commitment. Read this section and decide for yourself how our paragraph measures up according to these criteria. In which area is it strongest and in which is it weakest?

Escaping the "Badlands"

Have you ever finished a piece of writing, then read over your work, and finally, with profound critical insight, blurted out the word "blah"? Almost every writer feels that way sometime about his or her work. Some proceed to throw their work away. But that isn't necessary. With a little care, you can review your writing and single out any features that keep it in the "Badlands."

Here are six questions you can ask yourself when you review. By reviewing, you can catch opportunities you missed the first time around:

1. Is your topic worn-out?

2. Is your purpose stale?

3. Is your voice unnatural or fake?

4. Is your organization too predictable?

5. Is your focus unclear?

6. Do your sentences fall into a rut?

INSIDE

info

Notice, also, that these six are in descending order of importance. In other words, if your topic **(1)** is stale, don't worry yet about your organization **(4)** or your sentence structure **(6)**. If you change your topic, all of the next five aspects of your writing will change as well.

READ & REACT: Here's a challenge. Read the following paragraph, which most readers would probably consider boring, and examine each of the six aspects mentioned on the previous page until you've found the aspect that is most responsible for making it boring. Compare your reactions with someone else's. Then read the commentary below the paragraph. (No fair peeking!)

In today's society, there is much advertising to be found. You can find interesting ads in magazines, and there are commercials on TV about every ten minutes or so. A lot of people think the ads are better than the programs, and I kind of agree with them. Maybe that's why there are so many ads, because people like them. Someday maybe TV will be all ads and no programs. Would you like that?

6. Working up from the bottom of the list, notice that the **sentences** are in a rut. Almost all have uninteresting subjects and verbs, and too many clauses start with "there is" or "there are."

5. But the lack of **focus** is a bigger problem. Every sentence seems to have equal weight; therefore, none has special weight.

4. The **organization** is an even bigger problem: it goes from a vast generalization to general observations about what "a lot of people" think to a half-hearted question addressed to some nameless "you."

3. A bigger problem yet is the **voice**. It's tired, impersonal, and bored with its own subject. It has a short attention span.

2. Worse yet, the writer's **purpose** is weak and indefinite. The writer seems simply to be trying to get through an assignment.

1. Finally, and most boring of all, the writer's **topic** is too big, too ordinary, to be of any interest to a reader.

WRITE: Pretend the paragraph about advertising was your own first draft. Now that you've reviewed it and seen its problems, write a thorough revision, any length, about some aspect of advertising. Make your revision better than the original in all six areas; but this time, start improving from the **top** of the list (your topic) and work your way down.

Revising Texts

Questions for Revising

This checklist is for you if you've already written a first draft and done some revising, mostly rethinking your subject. In other words, your emphasis so far has been on thinking and expressing ideas. Now you are ready to take a closer look at your writing **as writing** and try to square away some important questions.

Four major questions to ask yourself:

1. Are there any places in my writing where I seem to forget the main thing I'm trying to do?

> **Comment:** Maybe you have not yet discovered the main thing you're trying to do. Or, if you have a main purpose, perhaps your attention wandered from it as you were writing.

> **Options:** (1) Cut out the excess material, or (2) tie it in somehow.

2. Is there any place in the text I haven't looked at closely enough?

> **Comment:** Looking closely at your subject can mean using extremely fine physical details. But it can also mean using pinpoint reasoning to explain your ideas.

> **Options:** (1) Add fine details, or (2) replace general language with detailed language. (Keep this in mind: General statements can get across only general ideas. Concretely detailed language gets across both the specifics and the overall picture.)

3. Is there any place where my readers need a statement of my meaning, my method, or my purpose?

> **Comment:** Sometimes a summarizing or organizing statement acts like a stone at the top of an archway—it keeps the rest of the stones from tumbling down. It may be the most important sentence you write.

> **Options:** (1) Provide a clear thesis statement, probably near the beginning. (2) Provide clear topic sentences. (3) If necessary, add whole paragraphs in longer pieces simply to explain what you're thinking, what you're doing, or where you're going next.

4. Have I written anything that didn't need to be written?

> **Comment:** This may be a problem with needless repetition. It may also be a problem with insulting the reader's intelligence—saying things that the reader probably already knows or could easily figure out.

> **Options:** Cut out the offending material and say, "Good riddance." (Warning: Be prepared to see some of your favorite words and phrases go!)

HANDBOOK HELPER: In the opening chapter in your handbook, you will find a more complete description of the entire writing process, from brainstorming to buffing. Pay especially close attention to the section labeled "Revising."

R-R-R-R-Revising

For revising early drafts, it helps to get into a rhythm of reading, thinking, and writing. Here is a five-step process that will help you catch the rhythm. Remember it by the 5 R's.

READ: To keep an open mind when you read what you have written, put some distance between yourself and your writing.

- If possible, put your writing aside for a day or two.
- Read it out loud, preferably in a private place where you can express yourself.
- Ask others (family, friends, classmates) to read it out loud to you. Listen to your own language: Does it sound like you? Can you understand it?
- Read it at different times of the day—moods can change.

REACT: Here are six questions that will help you react to your own writing on the second or third read-through:

- What parts of my writing work for me?
- Do all of these parts work together? Are they logical?
- Do all the parts somehow contribute to an overall idea or effect? What is it?
- Do the parts say exactly and only what I want them to say?
- Have I arranged the parts in the best possible order?
- What parts need the most improvement or a new direction?

REWORK: Next, based on your reactions to your own writing, revise it until all the parts work together well. You may spend a third or more of your writing time on this stage.

REFLECT: Now reflect on what you've done. It will help if you make comments in the margins of your paper. Here are some suggestions:

- Add exactly worded phrases and sentences to fill in areas where you need more information, more explanation, or more illustration.
- Use arrows to show exactly where a new passage should be inserted.
- Write down questions if you are not sure of the meaning or intention of a passage.
- Write notes to yourself, giving instructions for changes you want to make later.

REFINE: Refining is putting the final polish on your written copy. Here's what you can do:

- Once again, read your paper aloud, this time listening for glitches and looking for stylistic and mechanical improvements to make.

- Consult your handbook over questions of verb tense, subject/verb agreement, sentence structure, punctuation, and so on.

---

follow-up   Select a work in progress or a recently completed piece of writing. Review
→   this writing using the 5 R's as your guide.

Grand Openings

If an essay is like a tennis game, you don't have to start with a soft lob. You control the speed, and you control the spin. Suppose you've written an essay on a broad topic: "The Meaning of 'Family.'" Let's say this is how your first draft begins:

> The word "family" means many different things to many different people. Most people understand the meaning of family through their own experience, whether that is pleasant or unpleasant. My own experience was both pleasant and unpleasant.

Hmm. Maybe there is something interesting in that mixture of pleasant and unpleasant experience, but the writer hasn't given the reader a clue what it is.

READ & REACT: Below you'll find nine different ways to open an essay. Some name a type of opening and give you an example. Some name a type and let you make an example. And some ask you to think up both the type and an example. Fill in all the gaps.

Type of Opening	Example
1. A one-liner	As Martin Mull says, "Having a family is like having a bowling alley installed in your brain."
2. Exaggeration	I'm not saying my family was loud. But we were asked to build a high wood fence around our house so we wouldn't disturb the people at the airport.
• Try your own:	....
3. A rhetorical question	Is there any crisis in love or war that one is not prepared for by life in a family?
4. A brief story	
• Write one on your own paper.	

5. Dialogue

My little brother Ricky would do anything he could to get me in trouble. Here's how our conversations would sound.
"Hey, Ricky."
"Mom, Zelda's calling me names."
"I am not."
"And she keeps contradicting me."

- Try a dialogue of your own on your own paper.

6. Background

It took three generations to produce a family as tumultuous as ours. My paternal grandparents sit side by side in their old brown wedding pictures, as stiff as ventriloquists' dummies, only without the smiles. They had only one child, my father, who never spoke until he was three, and seldom thereafter. My mother's mother was the start of it all. Hotheaded, fun-loving, always gasping in surprise, even in her eighties when I knew her, she . . .

7. Analogy

Our family was the marching band of our neighborhood: big, booming, and always in rehearsal.

- Try your own: ....

....

8. Definition

"Family": an elaborate device for making adults out of children and children out of adults.

9. Make up a different kind of opening of your own

- Label it here: ....

- Give an example of it here: ....

....

follow-up Take one of your own pieces of writing—one that could use a wake-up call in the first sentence. Choose three of the types of openings mentioned above, and write three new openings for your essay. Then pick one of the three and keep going with it.

Refining:
Sentence Strengthening

Reviewing Sentence Types

Turn to "Structure of a Sentence," 759, in your handbook. There you'll find definitions and examples of four types of sentences:

● Simple   ● Compound   ● Complex   ● Compound-Complex

READ: Read and review the four types of sentences until you could explain each of them in detail to a younger person.

PRACTICE: Place the correct symbol (**S**, **Cp**, **Cx**, or **Cp-Cx**) in the space provided before each of the following sentences.

S = Simple	**Cx** = Complex
Cp = Compound	**Cp-Cx** = Compound-Complex

1. The curfew started in London, England, during the reign of King Alfred.

2. Wooden houses lined the streets of London, and fire was an ever-present danger.

3. An open fire burned in the center of every house or in its largest room.

4. When the church bells rang in the evening, it was a signal to cover the fire.

5. "Cover fire," which was slurred together in London speech, became "curfew," and the name stuck.

6. Curfew bells were discontinued when better building practices and better fire-fighting equipment were developed.

7. Today, curfews are used to help prevent "people" problems, not "fire" problems.

8. During riots and wars, curfews keep people who might cause trouble off the city streets.

9. Originally, the curfew meant "cover fire"; today, it means "cool it" to potential troublemakers.

follow-up
On your own paper, compose a paragraph that is exactly nine sentences long, on the topic of whether or not you should have an 11:00 p.m. curfew in your neighborhood. As you compose your sentences, follow exactly the sequence of sentence types you see as you read down the list of symbols you wrote above.

Adverb Clauses at Work

READ: The dependent clause is a <u>sub</u>ordinate clause. (*Sub* means *under or beneath*.) That means the dependent clause is subordinate or under the independent clause in importance. A complex sentence helps you tell the reader which of two ideas is the more important. The more important idea is placed in the independent clause. The less important idea is placed in the dependent, or subordinate, clause.

As you know, an adverb clause is a subordinate clause that can tell a number of things about the main idea such as *time*, the *reason why*, the *purpose or result*, or the *condition*.

<u>After the Civil War was over</u>, Washington, D.C., was still busy with political battles. (time)

<u>Since Edwin Stanton was Lincoln's secretary of war</u>, he came in for his share of political attacks. (reason why)

Northern sympathizers with the Southern cause were called "copperheads" <u>so that the name fit the venom of their tongues.</u> (purpose or result)

<u>Although words flew fast and furiously</u>, it was a cartoon that made a lasting contribution to our country's politics. (condition)

HANDBOOK HELPER: In your handbook, review the terms "clause," "adverb," and "subordinating conjunction" by looking them up in the index.

COMBINE: Combine each group of two simple sentences into a complex sentence by placing the less important idea in an adverb clause. An asterisk (*) is printed after the more important idea. In parentheses after each of your new complex sentences, explain what your adverb clause tells.

1. Thomas Nast created a cartoon with the Democrats pictured as a donkey.*
He wanted it to strike back against the attacks on Republican Edwin Stanton.

Because he wanted to strike back against the attacks on Republican Edwin Stanton,

Thomas Nast created a cartoon with the Democrats pictured as a donkey. (reason why)

2. Cartoonist Thomas Nast was defending Lincoln's secretary of war.
Nast pictured the secretary of war as a lion and the Democrats as a donkey.*

....

....

3. Opponents of the Democrats ridiculed the donkey symbol.
The donkey symbol was an overnight success.*

....

....

4. The Democrats did not create their donkey symbol.
The donkey is a permanent part of American politics.*

....

....

5. The Republicans adopted their elephant symbol four years later.*
The same cartoonist, Thomas Nast, gave the Republicans the idea.

....

....

6. Nast created a cartoon showing a berserk elephant labeled "Republican Vote."*
The Republicans were split over whom they should have as a presidential
candidate.

....

....

7. Thomas Nast was not complimenting the Republicans.
The elephant became the Republican's permanent symbol.*

....

....

Refining with Adverb Clauses

When you're a little child, ideas usually come to your mind one at a time:

> I want that ice-cream cone.

When you grow older, ideas may come in groups of two or three or more. And, as you speak or write, your mind is capable of sorting them in order of importance and linking them, putting some into main clauses and others into subordinate (or lesser) clauses, like this:

> If you're through licking that ice-cream cone, I want the leftovers so that I can curb my hunger pangs.

This sentence has two adverb clauses (subordinate clauses) that modify the verb in the main clause ("I want the leftovers").

Adverb clauses can be identified by the special function they serve and the distinctive words that introduce them:

- Some show the "time" of an idea related to the main idea. Watch for introductory words (called subordinating conjunctions) such as *before, after, when, until, since,* and *while.*

- Some show reasons "why." Watch for *because* and *since.*

- Some show "purpose" or "result." Watch for *that, so that,* and *in order that.*

- Some show "conditions." Watch for *if, unless, although, as long as,* and *even though.*

READ: Here is a short paragraph without any adverb clauses in it:

> The Converse Chuck Taylor All Star basketball shoe is an American classic. The company launched a series of TV spots. The shoe is less an athletic shoe than a fashion accessory.

REACT: Now turn the following sentences into adverb clauses and find a way to combine them with the main clauses in the paragraph above. For each adverb clause, use a subordinating conjunction that shows the relationship mentioned in parentheses. On your own paper, rewrite the whole paragraph, using adverb clauses effectively.

- It is now one of the cheapest shoes available. (*condition*)

- The company celebrated its 75th anniversary. (*time*)

- The public would continue to make the shoe its popular choice. (*purpose*)

- It was once the standard footwear of all self-respecting hoopsters. (*condition*)

Combining with Adjective Clauses

Sometimes a writer will wish to tuck a complete sentence into another sentence simply to modify one of the nouns. Note the basic sentence that follows:

The driver got a summons.

A modified version of this sentence, which gives you more exact information about both the driver and the summons, might sound like this:

The driver <u>who left her dented Firebird sports car under the tree</u> got a summons, <u>which will probably cost her a week's wages.</u>

The two groups of words underlined are both clauses that have been used to express subordinate ideas. Thus, they are called subordinate clauses. Since these clauses begin with relative pronouns (**who, which, that, whose, whom**), they are also called relative clauses. For a quick review of relative clauses, look up "Relative pronoun" in the index to your handbook.

WRITE: Read the following pairs of sentences. Figure out which one carries the main idea and which carries a subordinate idea. Then combine the two sentences, turning the subordinate sentence into a relative clause. Be sure to punctuate the sentence correctly.

1. A small contingent of the guests made fools of themselves.
The guests had been drinking prior to their arrival.

A small contingent of the guests, who had been drinking prior to their arrival, made fools of

themselves.

2. After 11:00 p.m. the people were arrested.
The people were making noise over 20 decibels.

3. I figured the comb did not belong to the policeman.
The policeman's hat had blown off, revealing a dome smoother than the gold one on the state capitol.

4. An experiment may not deserve federal funding.
The experiment does nothing to serve the public interest.

....

....

READ: Here is an assortment of sentences containing relative clauses. As you read them, circle the nouns modified by the relative clauses. Notice, in passing, how commas are used.

- Eagerness to read and correct student writing is not a (commodity) that grows on trees.

- Another reason why people who fish do not enjoy seeing water snakes is they think these snakes are aggressive.

- What is rigidly fixed is the path home, which follows the outward track in all its windings and all its crossings.

- I often marvel at certain types of bird behavior—flight, song, nest building, migration—that seem to me beyond explaining.

- The horse that comes in first can look forward to a life that is more pampered than that of its owner.

- She was seated next to that handsome man, whom she hated more than any other man alive.

- He was a man whose ego prevented him from enjoying the simple successes of others.

- This is my uncle, whose cabin in the woods has provided me with some of my most inspired hours.

INSIDE

info

Notice that if a relative clause is necessary to the definition of the noun it modifies (as in the sentence "She is the one who copied my project"), no comma or commas are needed to set it off. But if the relative clause offers an idea that is not necessary to the definition (as in the sentence "This is my only sister, who loves me unconditionally"), then a comma is needed. (For further examples, look up 586 in your handbook.)

Variety Is the Spice of Writing

Variety in sentence structure is essential to good writing. In the model below, Martha's message to Adam includes necessary information and is clear. However, the wordiness of the writing and the repetitive sentence structure detract from the message.

WRITE: On your own paper, revise the memo by cutting unnecessary words, combining some sentences, and beginning others with an introductory phrase or clause. For help, see the following sections in your handbook: "Primer Style" (060), "Adding Variety" (112), and "Transitions and Linking Words" (114).

Madison Avenue Mazda

Memo

Date: October 8, 1995

To: Adam Smith

From: Martha Southglow

Subject: Galen Harris's interview

Galen Harris came in this morning to interview for the position of service technician. He gave me a copy of his résumé. He described the work he has done in his part-time job at Leo's Tool Shed. He also described his student internship at Steffen's Implement. He talked about his training in the auto mechanics program at Kandiyohi Community College.

As the résumé illustrates, Mr. Harris has strong grade-point averages from Central High School and Kandiyohi. He has strong recommendations. He demonstrated good listening and speaking skills during the interview.

I've asked Mr. Harris to meet with you at 2:30 this afternoon in the Service Center. I would like you to talk with him about his knowledge of Mazdas. I would also like you to interview him regarding his experience working on Mazdas. Following your conversation, I would like you to call me to tell me whether you think we should hire Mr. Harris for the position.

Simply Dashing

The dash is a somewhat exotic punctuation mark, which, by its very nature, appears where one least expects it. There is no lengthy list of rules governing its use, as there is for the comma. Careful writers use dashes sparingly, usually to interrupt the expected flow of a sentence and show another layer of thought beneath or alongside the main point.

READ: Here are several "dashing" sentences by the wonderful Wyoming writer Gretel Ehrlich. She writes about the side of cowboys most people don't understand:

1. More often than not, circumstances—like the colt he's riding or an unexpected blizzard—are overpowering him.

2. In a rancher's world, courage has less to do with facing danger than with acting spontaneously—usually on behalf of an animal or another rider.

3. If a rancher or cowboy has been thought of as a "man's man"—laconic, hard-drinking, inscrutable—there's almost no place in which the balancing act between male and female, manliness and femininity, can be more natural.

4. What we've interpreted as toughness—weathered skin, calloused hands, a squint in the eye and a growl in the voice—only masks the tenderness inside.

5. So many of the men who came to the West were Southerners—men looking for work and a new life after the Civil War—that chivalrousness and strict codes of honor were soon thought of as western traits.

6. It's not that they're Jekyll and Hyde creatures—gentle with animals and rough on women—but rather, that they don't know how to bring their tenderness into the house.

REACT: Write full-sentence answers to these questions, which ask you to make observations about the sentences by Ehrlich:

● What would be the effect on these sentences if all the material between the dashes were dropped out? ....

....

● In most of these sentences, would commas work as well as dashes? Explain why or why not: ....

....

WRITE: From what you have observed about dashes by reading Ehrlich's sentences and by looking up "Dash" in the index of your handbook, write a paragraph for the benefit of one of next year's students explaining when and how and why to use dashes. In your paragraph, make sure that at least three of your sentences use dashes.

Again and Again

READ: Carefully read the following passage describing writer Willie Morris's childhood hometown (reprinted from his book *Good Old Boy*).

> . . . [Yazoo City] was a lazy town, stretched out on its hills and its flat streets in a summer sun; [it was] a dreamy place, always green and lush except for the four cold months at the beginning and end of each year. It was heavy with leafy smells, and in springtime there was a perfume in the air that made you dizzy if you breathed it too much. At night it was full of noises and lost ghosts—the witch in the cemetery who burned down the whole town in 1904, the giant-sized Indians buried in the Indian mounds, Casey Jones crashing into the freight train a few miles down the road. . . .

REACT: Each sentence in this description is constructed in much the same way, beginning with "Yazoo City was" or "It was" and following with similar-sounding, lush descriptions of the town. What effect does the repetition of the same basic sentence structure have on the writing? Does it make the description sound forceful and dramatic or poetic and dreamlike? What specific details help make the writing forceful or poetic? Discuss your ideas with a classmate.

WRITE: Complete the following writing frame patterned after the passage you have just read. Write the final copy of your work on your own paper. (Make adjustments to the frame below as necessary.) Share your results. **Special Note:** Make sure that you write from real experience.

.... is a .... town

(city, neighborhood, special meeting place, etc.); it is a(n) ....

place, always ....

It is .... ,

and in ....there is ....

At night, it is full of ....and .... —

....

INSIDE

info

One of the more effective ways to dramatize your thoughts and feelings is to present them in list form as you have done in this workshop. Readers and listeners naturally pick up on the rhythm, balance, and intensity this type of repetition produces.

Write in Style

An effective style in writing comes partly from choosing vivid verbs, concrete nouns, and figures of speech that convey living pictures as well as feelings.

READ: As you read the following paragraph about a New Yorker's Christmas in Honduras, try to be aware of any parts of it that strike you as effective style.

The cinder block walls of the living room were cold and unfriendly, and to a homesick twelve-year-old girl, they held no promise of a holiday celebration. The forlorn evergreen stood in the corner like a small student reprimanded for some childish error. Quietly, I tiptoed into the room, my eyes darting like two water bugs, searching the darkness for the lizards who would bed down here for the night. It would be a strange, silent Christmas here in poverty-stricken Honduras—far from the glamour of my home in New York. Slowly, I crept toward the electrical outlet and inserted the plug. A thousand brilliant jewels danced upon the tree, and from the darkness beyond the windows, a muffled gasp broke the silence. I looked out and found that I was not alone, for hand in hand around the living room windows stood the villagers, wonder and delight in their weary eyes.

REACT: After you have read it, go back into the paragraph and underline any words, passages, and figures of speech that you find interesting, pleasing, or surprising. See "Writing with Style" (058-068) in the handbook for more insights into effective writing style.

WRITE: Try to write a paragraph that you think has an even more interesting, smoother, or more colorful style than the one you've just read. Write about a memory of a time when you were in a strange place thinking of home. Show your paragraph to someone you trust and ask that person to comment on how effective your writing style is.

INSIDE

info

Not everything that draws attention to itself is "good style." In fact, some of the writers considered to be the best stylists write in an "invisible" style. That is, the thought always comes first, and the language, though it is colorful, never draws attention to itself for its own sake.

Words Have Feelings, Too

The **connotation** of a word is what it suggests or implies beyond its literal meaning. Careless writers sometimes lose sight of the connotations of their words and end up suggesting things they never intended. When you refine your writing, watch where your connotations are going. Better yet, take advantage of the possibilities for *coordinating* your connotations so that you subtly shape a reader's response.

READ & REACT: Fill in each blank in the paragraph below with the word from the list that best fits the meaning and feelings being communicated. (*Note:* Several words will work in each sentence; you must choose the word that best complements the tone the writer wants.)

Too many times I have picked up the evening newspaper to see a photograph of a very _____1._____-looking person splashed all over the front page. Usually, this person has just gone through a _____2._____ experience, like a car accident, a fire, or a shooting. You would think newspapers would use a little more _____3._____ and not choose such pictures to _____4._____ the front page of their papers. It's bad enough that these people have had to suffer a misfortune to begin with, and then to have their grief _____5._____ for everyone to see all seems very wrong. It _____6._____ their tragedy unnecessarily and makes it even more unlikely they will soon forget what has happened. They will be reminded over and over again by neighbors, friends, coworkers, and _____7._____ just how "terrible" and "awful" and "frightening" all of this must have been. They will be forced to _____8._____ an event weeks and months and perhaps years after it would otherwise have been forgotten. This is the power of the press—at its worst.

1. _____ (unhappy, miserable, distressed, tortured)

2. _____ (disagreeable, traumatic, bad, difficult)

3. _____ (discretion, intelligence, sensitivity, compassion)

4. _____ (brighten, appear on, emblazon, decorate)

5. _____ (shown, reproduced, advertised, broadcast)

6. _____ (inflates, builds up, supplements, exaggerates)

7. _____ (pals, well-wishers, troubled people, acquaintances)

8. _____ (relive, recall, remember, recollect)

Refining: Editing

Editing Checklist

Have you ever used a shopping or study list? Isn't it helpful to have your thoughts organized? The following checklist should help you each time you review and edit your writing. You might think of it as a "chopping" list, but it's really more: chopping, connecting, rearranging, polishing . . .

.... **1.** Read your final draft aloud to test it for sound and sense. Better yet, have someone read it aloud to you. Listen carefully as he or she reads. Your writing should read smoothly and naturally. If it doesn't, you have more editing to do.

.... **2.** Does each sentence express a complete thought? Does each paragraph have an overall point or purpose?

.... **3.** Have you used different sentence types and lengths? Are any sentences too long and rambling? Do you use too many short, choppy sentences?

.... **4.** Have you used a variety of sentence beginnings? Watch out for too many sentences that begin in exactly the same way.

.... **5.** Check each sentence for effective use of modifiers, especially prepositional phrases, participial phrases, and appositives. Have you punctuated these modifiers correctly?

.... **6.** Check your compound sentences. Do they contain two equal ideas, and is the logical relationship between the two ideas expressed by a proper conjunction (*and* versus *but* versus *or* . . .)?

.... **7.** What about your complex sentences? Have you used subordination effectively? Does the independent clause contain the most important idea? Are less important ideas contained in dependent clauses?

.... **8.** Make sure your writing is to the point. Have you avoided jargon, slang, redundancies, and other forms of wordiness?

.... **9.** Is your writing fresh and original? Have you avoided overused words and phrases? If not, substitute nouns, verbs, and adjectives that are specific, vivid, and colorful.

.... **10.** Replace any words or phrases that may be awkward, confusing, or misleading.

follow-up
Add points of your own so the list truly becomes a personal editing checklist. Then put the list to work. Choose a piece of unfinished writing and work with it, using the checklist as your guide.

Subject/Verb Agreement 1

In any survey of writing errors, subject/verb agreement errors always rank high. And why? We can thank compound subjects (*either Attila or the Huns*), indefinite pronouns (*neither*), and collective nouns (*species*) for part of the problem. When these types of words are used as subjects in sentences, it's not easy to determine if a verb should be singular or plural—*is* or *are, has* or *have,* etc. Note, for example, the following sentence:

Neither of the remaining Geo Storm cars (has, have) a red interior.

DISCUSS: The indefinite pronoun *neither* is the subject of this sentence. (Don't be fooled by *cars*. It is part of a prepositional phrase.) Which verb agrees in number with *neither*? *Have* sounds pretty good, doesn't it? But *neither* is a singular subject, and *have* happens to be a plural verb, so these two words can't agree in number. The correct answer is *has*—even though it may not sound right—because *has* is a singular verb. (*Neither of the remaining Geo Storm cars* **has** *a red interior.*) You can see why errors in agreement happen.

REACT: Take a few minutes to review the subject/verb agreement rules in the handbook (761-771). Then complete the following activity. Underline and label the subject (**S** for singular and **P** for plural) in each of the following sentences. Then circle the verb choice (in parentheses) that agrees with the subject in number.

1. The graduating <u>seniors</u> (is, are) now making important career decisions.
    [P label above "seniors"; "are" circled]

2. Anxiety and confusion (is, are) to be expected from these students as they make their choices.

3. Each of the government agencies (has, have) published a book of jobs available within that agency.

4. Occupational outlook books (is, are) published to help students with their career decisions.

5. Neither Rance nor his friend (is, are) going to a four-year college.

6. Many people (attends, attend) technical and specialty schools.

7. Both of Rance's parents (is, are) supportive of his decision.

8. Neither of Rance's counselors (was, were) aware of Rance's decision.

9. Everyone (was, were) anxious to hear which school Alex decided to attend.

10. Alex as well as his parents (is, are) happy with his choice—the University of Hawaii.

Subject/Verb Agreement 2

READ: In each sentence below, underline the subject and circle the verb choice (in parentheses) that agrees in number with the subject.

1. The first <u>day</u> of speech class (is, are) often a little frightening.

2. Each of the students (is, are) required to give eight speeches throughout the semester.

3. Of the eight speeches that are assigned, the first (is, are) the easiest to write and the most difficult to present.

4. All of the speakers (is, are) to be prepared on the same day.

5. Either Joanna or Joyce (is, are) to give her first speech today.

6. Economics (is, are) the topic of Joanna's speech.

7. Half of the students (is, are) scheduled to present speeches today.

8. Someone in the class (is, are) snickering as Joanna is giving her speech.

9. Joanna does a good job in spite of the distraction and (hope, hopes) to receive a strong evaluation.

10. Each member of the class (write, writes) a critique of each presentation.

11. The speech faculty (establishes, establish) the criteria for the evaluation of the speakers.

12. Neither Royce nor Angela (is, are) anxious to stand in front of the class.

13. Most of the class members (pick, picks) subjects that are interesting to them.

---

follow-up Use each of the following italicized words as the subject in a sentence. (Use your own paper for your work.) Upon completion, exchange your sentences with a classmate, and check each other's work for subject/verb agreement.

- The indefinite pronoun **everybody**
- The indefinite pronoun **all** as a plural subject
- The collective noun **crowd** as a singular subject
- **Athletics** as a subject referring to activities
- A compound subject connected by **or**

Better Left Unsaid

REACT: Make the following sentences more concise by eliminating *deadwood*, *redundancy*, and other *wordiness*. For clear definitions of each of these terms, consult the index to your handbook. Place parentheses around any unnecessary words or phrases that you find.

1. The former tenant who had lived in the apartment before we moved in painted all the walls with a coat of pink paint.

2. The length of the average basketball court is normally 90 feet long.

3. The main reason he didn't pass the test is because he didn't study carefully or look over his class notes.

4. There are six students who volunteered on their own to clean up after the homecoming dance is over.

5. The mountain climber was unable to descend down the mountain by himself and needed the help of another climber to assist him.

6. The fragile vase, which would surely break if mishandled, was shipped "Special Handling" so that it would be handled with care.

7. The canceled game has been rescheduled for 8:00 p.m. tomorrow evening.

8. A portable radio can be carried anywhere and is especially handy for jogging, biking, and other outdoor activities.

9. As a general rule, he usually spends about one hour of his time each day reading.

10. Needless to say, wordiness is a writing problem that should be eliminated from all writing, which goes without saying.

Psst! Compare your answers with a partner's. See who was able to remove the most words without changing the basic sense of the sentences.

Hanging Out

READ: What is wrong with the following sentence?

> After finishing her routine on the parallel bars, the judge gave Juanita the winning score.

It sounds as if the judge herself finished the routine, instead of Juanita. Why? Because of a mistake in the way the sentence is worded.

● To correct the mistake, we could change the opening phrase:

> After Juanita finished her routine on the parallel bars, the judge gave her a perfect score.

● We could also change the main clause:

> After finishing her routine on the parallel bars, Juanita was given a perfect score by the judge.

When a modifying phrase at the opening of a sentence does not match the subject of the sentence, it is called a *dangling modifier*. Dangling modifiers are a serious writing problem because they destroy the logic of a writer's statement.

HANDBOOK HELPER: Look up dangling modifiers in your handbook (088). Then look up verbals in your handbook (737). There you will find a description of three types of verbals: gerunds, infinitives, and participles. These three types of verbals are often found in dangling modifiers. Learn to recognize them and to understand the implied subject of the verbal. That will make fixing, or editing, dangling modifiers easier.

CORRECT the following sentences by rewording either the modifying opening phrase or the main clause. If the sentence is already correct, place a *C* on the line.

1. Using a computer to help diagnose engine problems, the car was expertly repaired by our mechanic.

Using a computer to help diagnose engine problems, our mechanic expertly repaired

the car.

2. While playing the piano, our dog began to howl at me.

3. After writing spontaneously for half an hour, our teacher said we should gather in small groups to discuss our drafts.

4. Scanning the horizon, we spotted a faint plume of smoke.

5. To seal the bargain, the grocer and the supplier shook hands.

6. Afraid to look, the bobcat made Thurgood tremble with fear.

7. After finishing the first three courses of our meal, the server brought out the dessert tray.

8. Whipping the willow's branches back and forth, we huddled at the screen door to watch the wind.

Psst! Always check your writing for phrase modifiers that are incorrectly "hanging out." They will destroy the logic of your ideas and weaken the overall effect of your work.

Let Me Make This Perfectly Clear

Lack of clarity in writing can be caused by a number of problems:

- misplaced modifiers
- mixed constructions
- incomplete comparisons
- substandard language
- double negatives

Your job as an editor is to understand these problems, to spot them in sentences, and to fix them. Your handbook can help you do this. Look for examples and explanations of all of these problems in your handbook, 069-101.

DIRECTIONS: In the space before each of the following sentences, label the type of stylistic problem you find in the sentence. In the space after the sentence, rewrite the sentence in a corrected form. Reword or rephrase if necessary.

Problem:	Sentence:
incomplete comparison	**1.** Jordana gives more time and attention to English class than her friends. Jordana gives more time and attention to English class than her friends do.
	2. A time warp is when something is displaced from one point in time to another, as in science-fiction stories. (Hint: Is "time warp" a thing or an occasion?)
	3. The reason he did not make it on time is because he lost his watch. (Hint: Do you need both "the reason" and "because"?)

Problem: **Sentence:**

....   **4.** It would of worked out better if we could all have gone with you.

....

....

                                (*Hint:* Would you speak or write this way on a formal occasion?)

....   **5.** I will give you a better deal on a watch than Tom.

....

....

                                (*Hint:* Does this one remind you of one of the previous sentences?)

....   **6.** Always try and be on time, especially if others have to wait on you.

....

....

                                (*Hint:* Do you see a place where an infinitive would be appropriate?)

....   **7.** Nobody in his or her right mind wouldn't do a foolish thing like that.

....

....

....   **8.** Mom fixed several snacks for the children with a variety of healthful ingredients.

....

....

                                (*Hint:* Just which "healthful ingredients" do children contain?)

....   **9.** After helping to get his younger brothers and sisters ready for school, Jose couldn't hardly make it to work on time.

....

....

....   **10.** That painting is my favorite piece in the entire gallery with the fluorescent colors.

....

....

Pronoun Problems

A pronoun is like the jacket you leave on a seat at a concert to show that the seat is saved. The jacket is not the person; it stands in place of the person. In the same way, a pronoun is not a noun; it stands in place of a noun, which is referred to as its "antecedent."

A pronoun works well when both the writer and the reader can tell exactly which word is its antecedent. But read the following sentence and notice the problem with one of the pronouns and its antecedent:

As she edged her car toward the drive-up window, it made a strange rattling sound.
(Does "it" refer to the car or to the window?)

This is an example of **indefinite pronoun reference**. The pronoun could be referring to either of two words in the sentence.

To correct sentences like this, it is usually best to replace the indefinite pronoun with a noun, depending upon the meaning you wish to convey. (Rephrasing the sentences is also acceptable.) Here are two ways to correct the sample sentence:

As she edged her car toward the drive-up window, the car made a strange rattling sound.

As she edged toward the drive-up window, her car made a strange rattling sound.

CHALLENGE: Each of the following sentences has an indefinite pronoun in it. Using the lines provided, correct each sentence so its meaning is clear.

1. The team moved the wrestling mat off the gym floor so that it could be cleaned.

....

....

....

2. When Tara entered her program into the computer, it went completely haywire.

....

....

....

3. Alina asked her mother if she could carry one of the boxes for her.

....

....

....

4. Frank let Carlos know that his microphone wasn't working.

....

....

....

5. Check all your papers for careless writing errors so that your teacher can enjoy . . reading them.

....

....

....

6. Shortly after the old car had been given a final coat of paint, it began to run.

....

....

....

follow-up   Write three sentences that contain indefinite pronoun references. Exchange
your work with a classmate, and correct each other's sentences.

Sentence Errors

With a few exceptions in special situations, you should use complete sentences when you write. By definition, a complete sentence expresses a complete thought. Among the most common errors made when attempting to write complete (and effective) sentences are fragments, comma splices, and run-ons. (Review these errors in your handbook if you're not sure which is which.)

READ: After reading the following paragraph, identify each numbered group of words as a complete sentence (**S**), a sentence fragment (**F**), a comma splice (**CS**), or a run-on sentence (**RO**). (Use the spaces following the paragraph for your answers.) Rewrite the paragraph on your own paper, making the necessary changes to correct the sentence errors.

1My neighbor, Mrs. Cape, who is Italian. 2Still finds it difficult to understand her husband's English accent. 3He was born in Liverpool, England, but came to the United States in 1960. 4He's obviously been here quite a long time, however, he still has a strong accent. 5Especially when he's mad. 6Have you ever heard John Cleese of *Fawlty Towers* fame once he's warmed up, then you know how Mr. Cape can sound. 7Mrs. Cape isn't much better; she starts jabbering in lightning-speed Italian when she gets upset. 8Things really get hilarious when both of them get excited. 9One of them will say something nearly incomprehensible, and the other one quickly responds with his or her own jibberish. 10Back and forth they go. 11Without really seeming to know what each other is saying half the time. 12They each want to get the last word in. 13If you were to visit their apartment during one of these "discussions," you'd be sure to go away with a new appreciation of the power of language. 14As for Mr. and Mrs. Cape. 15Their linguistic differences simply add a healthy dose of diversity to their lives.

1. _____ 2. _____ 3. _____ 4. _____

5. _____ 6. _____ 7. _____ 8. _____

9. _____ 10. _____ 11. _____ 12. _____

13. _____ 14. _____ 15. _____

INSIDE info

In the "Writing with Style" section of the handbook, where sentence errors are discussed, you will find information related to writing clear, concise, smooth, and logical sentences. Think of this section as your complete guide to improving sentence style. Refer to it regularly.

Sentence Fragments: Uses and Abuses

From elementary school onward, you've been told to avoid writing sentence fragments, as if all fragments are the result of stupid mistakes. Strange. Lots of published writing contains fragments. It appears that some fragments are written on purpose.

READ: Here is a paragraph with some accidental fragments in it (see the italicized words). Read it carefully. Then in the space provided below, change each fragment into a complete, effective sentence. (Refer to "Fragment sentence" in the handbook index for help.)

Both pleasant and unpleasant situations can cause stress. *Any incident that places a demand on you to readjust or change.* The reaction of the physical body to stress is the same. *Whether the stressor is pleasant or unpleasant.* A person can be completely free of stress. *But only after he or she dies.*

1. ....

....

2. ....

....

3. ....

....

READ & REACT: Here are some passages in which the writer deliberately uses fragments (in italics) for stylistic purposes. As you read these passages, determine the purpose of each fragment and how well each one works.

- Everyone in that family, including my three cousins, could draw a horse. *Beautifully.*
  —Annie Dillard

- Mrs. Stokes: Weezie, come get your lunch, girl.
  Weezie: *No time. Lots of homework.*

- *A place to rest in the middle of the lagoon. Drips from the oars.* An egret flaps its wings where it stands.

EDIT: Here is a paragraph that contains a few deliberate and a few accidental fragments. Underline the deliberate fragments but *edit* (correct) all the accidental ones.

Time for recreation to ease your mind. Physical exercise to relieve physical and mental tension. Having a job that you enjoy, that you feel well-equipped to perform, and that others appreciate. These are a few of the keys to managing stress. But notice that recreation, physical exercise, and work are stressors in themselves. Dr. Selye, a physician from Montreal, Canada, who has authored several books on stress. Says that the reaction of the body to stress is the same. Whether the stressor is pleasant or unpleasant. Generally speaking, stress makes life more interesting. A person free from stress only when he or she dies. However, a type of stress called "distress" is harmful. Potentially. Distress can be caused by a daily job. That you dislike immensely. If you can exchange a distressing job for a more satisfying one. Do it. If not, talk over the pressures of work. With someone you trust and respect. Try to accept what you cannot change. And remember to leave time. For exercise and rest.

follow-up Write a short paragraph on any topic. Purposely use a few fragments for special effect.

Refining: Proofreading

Proofreading Checklist

The following guidelines will help you put the finishing touches on your writing before you share it with your readers. (As you use this checklist, add points of your own to truly make it a personal checklist.)

Spelling

1. Have you spelled all your words correctly? Here are some tips:

- Read your writing backward and aloud—one word at a time—so you focus on each word.
- Circle each word you are unsure of.
- For help, consult the list of commonly misspelled words in your handbook. (For additional help, check a dictionary.)

Punctuation

2. Does each sentence end with a punctuation mark?

3. Are coordinating conjunctions (*and, but, or, so*, etc.) in compound sentences preceded by a comma? Have you used commas to set off items listed in a series, after introductory clauses, . . .?

4. Have you used apostrophes to show possession or to mark contractions?

5. Is all dialogue or written conversation properly punctuated?

Capitalization

6. Do all sentences (dialogue) begin with a capital letter?

7. Have you capitalized the proper names of people, places, and things?

Usage

8. Have you misused any of the commonly mixed pairs of words: *there / their / they're; accept / except?* Refer to the section "Using the Right Word" in your handbook.

9. Have you used any words, phrases, or sentences that may confuse the reader?

Grammar

10. Do your subjects and verbs agree in number?

11. Do your pronouns agree with their antecedents?

12. Have you used any sentence fragments, run-ons, or rambling sentences?

Form

13. Have you chosen an appropriate title if one is needed?

14. Is your paper labeled correctly with your name and class?

15. Does the form of the writing fit the assignment?

Common Errors

IDENTIFY: Proofread the paragraph below, looking for errors in capitalization, abbreviations, numbers, and punctuation. Draw a line through any word, number, or abbreviation that is used incorrectly and write the correct form above each error. Add (or take out) punctuation as necessary.

1   Have you ever known a person who was completely unpredictable? We had

2   a neighbor once who seemed to have ~~2~~ two personalities that switched on and off

3   like hot and cold running water. it was always one extreme or the other. His

4   name was mister Bunde, and he was our next-door neighbor when we lived on

5   south maple st. I worked for him one Summer while I was in grade school,

6   cutting his lawn and doing his other yard work. After one summer though I'd

7   had enough. Even if he hadn't moved that november I wouldn't have worked

8   for him again, no matter how much he paid me! In general he tried to be a nice

9   guy, and he liked to joke but it was difficult to tell if he was really kidding or

10   if his mood had suddenly changed. When it did things were unbelievably

11   difficult. I couldn't do anything right and he would complain about some of the

12   silliest and most unimportant things imaginable. Sometimes mr bunde

13   complained about other neighbors and he would expect me to agree with him

14   even though he knew they were my friends. Then in another minute he would

15   be kidding again being overly friendly and clever. It was very difficult working

16   with someone so unpredictable. I not only had my work to concentrate on, but

17   I also had to be constantly on my guard trying to predict Mr. Bunde's moods

18   and stay 1 step ahead of him.

---

follow-up Now that you are an expert, what suggestions would you have for someone
who is just beginning to work on his or her proofreading skills?

The Capital Steps

IDENTIFY: Test your skill as a proofreader in the paragraphs below. Capitalize each letter that should be capitalized, punctuate or write out each abbreviation, use numerals or spelled-out numbers properly, and add or change punctuation as necessary.

1   **H**
     Have you ever traveled to another country. I know from personal experience

2   that living abroad can be an exciting and memorable adventure when I was

3   twelve years old my family spent 6 months in london england. we lived in a

4   small Flat in kensington gardens, kensington gardens is close to london the

5   financial and fashion center of england.

6   london is a fascinating city, it is filled with historical buildings such as the

7   houses of parliament the british museum and st pauls cathedral moreover it is

8   home to cultural sites such as the royal academy of arts. During our 6 month

9   stay my family spent countless hours walking through the british museum

10   riding the double-decker buses and retracing the steps of famous british poets

11   and writers. it was in london that I 1st discovered the differences between

12   american english and the queens english.

13   My introduction to the queens english was swift and confusing one day I

14   started out for the british museum but I got lost looking for the train. I stopped

15   a distinguished looking gentleman and asked him where I might find the train.

16   Train? he asked, looking confused.

17   yes, train. you know it goes underground . . . choo-choo, I replied.

18   He scratched his head, then said, train? Are you sure?

19   Yes, I replied. I know there's one nearby.

20   Suddenly he brightened. Ah, yes indeed, the tube.

21   Tube, I asked.

22   He smiled wisely. My dear young man in england its called the tube.

23   There were many other times I felt betrayed by my native language the

24   british say lift for elevator biscuits for cookies bumpershoot for umbrella. In

25   short, theirs is a very confusing english.

26   Although the language is confusing the weather often rainy and the food

27   different london is a magical city. The city itself dates back to the second

28   century and parts of londons early city can be seen in fragments of roman brick

29   that are visible in the walls of the tower of london. history buffs enjoy tracing

30   the citys development and growth during walking tours these tours take you

31   through covent garden the chief flower and fruit market fleet street the center

32   of londons newspaper industry and buckingham palace where one can still

33   witness the changing of the guard. London is a very special city and deserves

34   a leisurely visit I'm glad I was able to spend this time in another country. Its

35   a time I'll never forget

INSIDE Do you know which words in a title should be capitalized? Do you know the difference between an *acronym* and an *initialism*? And do you know how to express very large numbers in your writing? You'll find answers to these questions (and any other question you have about capitalization, abbreviations, and numbers) in your handbook. (Refer to "Checking Mechanics," 652-691, in the Proofreader's Guide.)

Reviewing Comma Rules

IDENTIFY: Complete each of the comma rules below by inserting the correct word(s). Try to do it without looking in your handbook; then double-check your answers using your handbook and correct any rules you may have gotten wrong. Apply each rule by inserting needed commas in the sample sentence.

1. Commas are used to enclose a title or .... and ....

that follow a surname.

   Lawrence, D. H. White E. B. and Chesterton G. K. are famous writers.

2. Use a comma to separate contrasted .... from the rest of the
   sentence.

   A peanut is actually a legume not a nut.

3. A comma is used to separate an .... clause or a long modifying

phrase from the independent clause that follows it.

   While it may be hard to believe the average person ingests about a ton of food and

   drink each year.

4. Commas are used to separate a vocative (a vocative is the .... that

names the person or persons spoken to) from the rest of the sentence.

   Did you know Karen that Wyoming was the first state to allow women to vote?

5. Commas are used to separate a series of .... in order to distinguish

hundreds, thousands, millions, etc.

   There are nearly 250000 species of beetles on the earth.

6. A comma is used between two .... clauses that are joined by

coordinating conjunctions such as these: *but, or, nor, for, yet, and, so.*

   Samuel Taylor Coleridge was in the middle of writing down the visions he had seen

   in a dream when someone knocked on his door and he rose to let the person in.

7. Commas are used to enclose .... phrases and clauses.

Coleridge who later returned to his work could not remember the rest of his dream.

8. Commas are used to set off the .... words of the speaker from t

the rest of the sentence.

"This is why" explained Miss Jackson "the famous poem 'Kubla Khan' remains

unfinished."

9. Commas are used to separate individual words, phrases, or clauses in a ....

James Madison Theodore Roosevelt Abraham Lincoln and Ulysses S. Grant

were all presidents of the United States.

10. Commas are used to separate items in an .... and items in a

....

On January 20 1953 former president Dwight D. Eisenhower moved to 1600

Pennsylvania Avenue Washington D.C.

11. Commas are used to set off a word, phrase, or clause that ....the

movement of the sentence.

We toured several rooms on the first floor of the White House; we did not however

get to see the president's living quarters on the second and third floors.

12. Commas are used to separate coordinate adjectives that .... modify

the same noun.

The magnificent towering Washington Monument draws some two million visitors

each year.

13. A comma is used to separate an ....or a weak exclamation

from the rest of the sentence.

Wow that's a lot of people!

Multiple Choice

IDENTIFY: Study the comma rules in your handbook. Select the correctly punctuated sentence from each group below. Write the letter of the correct sentence on the blank before each group. On the lines below each group, explain why your choice is the only correct one. (*Note:* The multiple choice form used below is often found on ACT and SAT exams.)

1. A. John has been going to school at Mt. Pleasant High School, 232 Selby Road, Mt. Pleasant, Vermont 10523, since September 1990.
   B. John has been going to school at Mt. Pleasant High School, 232 Selby Road, Mt. Pleasant, Vermont, 10523, since September 1990.
   C. John has been going to school at Mt. Pleasant High School, 232 Selby Road, Mt. Pleasant, Vermont 10523 since September, 1990.

....

....

2. A. "This fall," John's mother said with pride in her voice "my son will be going to Stanford University in California."
   B. "This fall," John's mother said with pride in her voice, "my son will be going to Stanford University in California."
   C. "This fall" John's mother said with pride in her voice, "my son will be going to Stanford University in California."

....

....

3. A. One day if all goes as planned, John will be known as John Kemper, M.D.
   B. One day, if all goes as planned, John will be known as John Kemper M.D.
   C. One day, if all goes as planned, John will be known as John Kemper, M.D.

....

....

4. A. Do you realize John, that you will have a considerably larger workload in college than you had in high school?
   B. Do you realize, John, that you will have a considerably larger workload in college than you had in high school?
   C. Do you realize, John that you will have a considerably larger workload in college than you had in high school?

....

....

And to quote . . .

IDENTIFY: Add quotation marks where they are needed. Underline words that should be in italics. (Refer to the "Marking Punctuation" section of your handbook, 575-651, for help.)

1. Did she discuss Whittier's poem The Eternal Goodness?

2. Brahma has four stanzas; each stanza contains four lines.

3. Age of Gold is a phrase in Emerson's poem Character.

4. The Latin word ibidem means in the same place.

5. Ibid. is the abbreviated form sometimes used in footnotes.

6. Please don't stare at me like that! she snapped.

7. Who's staring at you? he asked.

8. My young man, Mr. Langdon said, please concentrate on one thing at a time. Either listen or talk, but don't try to do both.

9. Improvisation for the Theatre is a fine book written by Viola Spolin.

10. Jeff forgot to ask whether the Kansas City Clipper had sailed out this morning.

11. Miss Vanden Berg asked, Did you ever read London's story To Build a Fire ?

12. No! Angela exclaimed. But I did finish Addison's essay Sir Roger and the Witches!

13. The only narrative poem Carmen read is Old Christmas; Sweet and Low is a lyric poem, not a narrative poem.

14. My mother subscribes to both Time and Newsweek.

15. Mr. Ryken's conversation is always sprinkled with ah's and ahem's.

16. In 1955, four different singers recorded the same song. Amazingly, all four versions of It's Almost Tomorrow made the Top Forty.

17. The best-selling rock single is one that is still timely today: Rock Around the Clock. To date, it has sold over 25 million copies.

"Look at semicolons and love them . . ."

"Look at semicolons ;;;;;;;;;;;;;;;;;;;; and love them, because they can be a master key to the American punctuation system. Consider this mark ; —a period above a comma. You'd expect it to be a stronger mark than the comma, and it is." So says writer and teacher Ken Macrorie in his book *Searching Writing*. He goes on to ask an important question: "But how do we learn the semicolon's several uses?" That is the question we will explore in this activity.

REACT: Team up with a classmate to study the following sets of statements containing semicolons. (Each set of sentences uses semicolons in a different way.) Then develop a rule explaining how semicolons are used in each of the three sets. (No peeking in the handbook until after you've finished.)

Set 1

I once had a '55 Chevy with a 283; that was the first V-8 I ever owned.

The venom from the king cobra is the most deadly of all snake poisons; a single gram can kill 150 people.

Black holes are areas in which gravity is extremely strong; anything pulled into the black hole cannot get out.

(*Hints:* Study the groups of words before and after the semicolons. What do these groups of words have in common? Can they stand alone? What other punctuation marks could be used in place of the semicolons?)

Rule: ....

....

Set 2

I packed a razor, toothbrush, and deodorant; blue jeans, bathing suit, and jacket; tennis balls, fishhooks, and golf clubs.

For the food drive the store owner provided canned soups, vegetables, and meats; packaged breads, rolls, and cookies; assorted fruits, nuts, and mixes.

(*Hint:* Note that each sentence contains a related series of items. How are semicolons used in relation to the different series of items?)

Rule: ....

....

Set 3

A shark has a built-in immunity to nearly every type of bacteria; consequently, it almost never gets sick.

The Chicago Cubs are seen across the country on cable television; as a result, they are one of the most popular baseball teams in America.

The dinner at the banquet was disappointing; however, the entertainment that followed made up for the lumpy mashed potatoes and rubbery chicken.

(*Hints:* Pay special attention to the words or phrases immediately following the semicolons. What do they have in common? What function do they serve? What additional punctuation mark appears within each sentence?

Rule: ....

....

REVIEW: Compare your rules with a classmate's rules. Also compare your work with the rules for using semicolons as stated in the handbook. (Refer to "Semicolon" in the handbook, 595-598.) If any of your explanations are too far off the mark, revise them accordingly.

DISCUSS: Now that you've studied semicolons, why do you think Mr. Macrorie calls this mark the "master key" to punctuation? Is he right?

---

follow-up Write freely about planning a meeting, learning a lesson, making a big mistake, or a subject of your own choosing. Make sure you use semicolons in at least two different ways in your writing.

Punctuation Review

IDENTIFY: Read each of the following sentences carefully. Circle the letter in front of each sentence that is correctly punctuated. Place an X over the letter in front of each sentence that has an error in punctuation.

1. **A.** Elaine plays the flute and she sings in the chorus.

B. Elaine plays the flute, and she sings in the chorus.

C. Elaine plays the flute and sings in the chorus.

D. Elaine plays the flute; she also sings in the chorus.

E. Elaine plays the flute not the clarinet in the orchestra.

F. Elaine, a talented singer, has a solo in the spring concert.

G. After years of lessons and practice, Elaine will have the chance to show her talent in front of a large audience.

H. When the concert is over Elaine will have accomplished one of her goals.

I. Elaine will have accomplished one of her goals when the concert is over.

J. The concert will be held on Friday, April 6, in the school auditorium at 7:30 p.m.

2. **A.** Roger and Randy are twins; they were born in September 1979.

B. Teachers often have trouble knowing which one is Roger and which one is Randy, but their close friends can easily tell the difference.

C. Randy has a wider smile talks louder and walks faster.

D. Roger likes: bowling, snowmobiling, and basketball.

E. Randy prefers these sports: swimming, football, and skiing.

3. **A.** Marsha doesn't like to get up in the morning she'd rather sleep until noon.

B. Marsha's mother said that "Marsha is lazy."

C. Marsha objected to the word "lazy."

D. "Mom, I'm just a night person," explained Marsha.

E. "Yes, replied her mother, but the world runs on daylight savings time!"

IDENTIFY: In the sentences below, commas, semicolons, quotation marks, and apostrophes have been left out. Fill in punctuation marks as needed *before*, *in*, or *after* the underlined words. Please print your answers carefully, showing exactly where each punctuation mark belongs. (*Note:* Not all underlined words need punctuating.)

1   Warren Zeeger a future newspaperman likes to go to fires listen to police calls and
2   take photos of his high schools athletic events. Warrens dreams center on earning his
3   days wages as a foreign correspondent. He wants to take off for far-off places packing
4   only a toothbrush and razor a sport coat, trench coat, and tuxedo, pencils, paper, and
5   portable typewriter. Isabel who is older says that Warren's dreams are unrealistic
6   nevertheless if you don't have a dream you dont have a direction for your life. As Warren
7   once said I'm not going to drift through life. Im going to go for it!
8   Did you say, Go for it? asked Isabel as she stuffed another candy bar in her mouth
9   and turned up the Saturday morning cartoons on her mother-in-laws television set.

10   If Doris plans change she will not be able to join us. Yes Doris had to change her
11 plans she will not join us.

12   When they had enough money the three boys put their savings together and
13 bought a boat. It was Leroy Les and Larrys boat. The boat cost $1436. They kept the
14 boat at Amos Marina, 231 West Gull Road Memphis Tennessee during the summer and
15 in Les garage in the winter.

16   Washington Irving who was born on April 3 1783 was the first American writer to
17 create literature of lasting artistic value. Irving is best known today for two short stories
18 The Legend of Sleepy Hollow and Rip Van Winkle.
19   Rip Van Winkles long sleep Is part of the American literary heritage. Lazy good-
20 natured Rip had a scolding wife. Rip had to escape and he did. Rip took his gun and his
21 dog and he wandered through the nearby Catskill Mountains. Rip helped an old gnomelike
22 stranger who was struggling with a keg and was invited to join a party of little men playing
23 at ninepins and drinking. After the party was over Rip fell asleep.   He slept for twenty
24 years he slept straight through the American Revolution. Obviously many things had
25 changed when Rip finally awoke.

Usage

IDENTIFY: Read each of the sentences below very carefully. Underline the correct choice within each set of parentheses. (Refer to the "Using the Right Word" section in your handbook.)

1. "(It's, Its) not an easy decision!" Avery cried in dismay.

2. Avery Jones is having (a lot, alot) of difficulty making a career decision.

3. (All ready, Already) Avery has made the decision to (further, farther) his education.

4. Avery's morale was boosted when he learned of the (number, amount) of people having the same difficulty.

5. Avery has researched (quiet, quit, quite) a few of the options.

6. (Among, Between) these options is the career decision for Avery.

7. "(Who's, Whose) decision is it anyhow?" Avery asked his parents.

8. "(It's, Its) (your, you're) decision to make, Avery," replied his parents.

9. Realizing that this is a (very, real) important decision, Avery did not (lose, loose) sight of his (personal, personnel) interests.

10. "(Besides, Beside), we would rather have you do what you want (then, than) what you think we want," Avery's parents continued.

11. Avery (sat, set) down with some (stationary, stationery) and made a list of his high-school courses.

12. Avery (complemented, complimented) himself on his many interests.

13. (Later, Latter) that day Avery decided to seek (counsel, council) concerning his career decision.

14. (Fewer, Less) students are seeking help from counselors (then, than) ever before, he was told.

15. The (affect, effect) the counselor had on Avery was quite amazing.

16. Avery began to (accept, except) the fact that he was (disinterested, uninterested) in college.

17. "College is great," he told a friend, "but I must (chose, choose) a career that (compliments, complements) both my interests and abilities."

18. In the (past, passed) year, quite a few of Avery's friends have decided which (course, coarse) they want to follow.

19. Avery's friends said (their, there, they're) decisions were all based on (personal, personnel) preference rather (then, than) peer pressure.

20. Avery had no (allusions, illusions) about the work that would be involved.

21. (There, Their, They're) are (alot, a lot) of eminent instructors teaching at the vocational school Avery (chose, choose).

follow-up Write a paragraph on a topic of your own choice, making 6-10 deliberate usage mistakes. Choose your words from the listing of commonly mixed pairs in your handbook (692-701). Then exchange your work with a classmate, challenging each other to find and correct the usage errors.

What's the Usage?

PROOFREAD: Proofread the paragraphs below, looking for errors in usage. Draw a line through any word used incorrectly and write the correct word above it. (Refer to the "Using the Right Word" section in your handbook for help.)

1 The teachers in Rock River have chosen to picket the administration building as a

2 last coarse of action to resolve the stalemate in contract talks. Radio, TV, and newspaper

3 stories covered the event continually [at regular intervals]: "Teachers Demand to Be Herd";

4 "Tempers Flare in Contract Talks"; "Town Counsel Calls for Settlement."

5 It was a chilly December morning, and Zig Koscinski, a math teacher in neighboring

6 Raymond, had been chosen by his Education Association to help the Rock River teachers

7 gain support. It was 8:00 a.m. and the city streets were nearly deserted, but their was

8 hardly any room to move in the old, abandoned store that served as a meeting hall for the

9 teachers and their supporters. Zig and other teachers who had been scent to support the

10 educators picked up their picket signs and stepped out of the old store onto the main street

11 of town. "Ah," thought Zig, "it's a cold morning alright, but not to cold to work." He pushed

12 his sign high in the air. "I haven't felt such a brisk breeze since I emigrated from Poland

13 in '74," he thought.

14 Just then, a picketer joined Zig. It was clear by her expression that she really wanted

15 know part of picketing. "Isn't this hole business a terrible mess? My association choose

16 me to come today, but I wish I had stayed home." She attempted to hide her sign behind

17 her arms. "How do we think we can heel discord by walking down the street with these

18 silly signs? Its just not worth it."

follow-up There are more than 100 commonly mixed pairs listed in your handbook. Review this list and find the words that you commonly misuse in your writing. On your own paper, list four pairs of words that always seem to give you problems. Try to explain the difference *between* (or *among*) the words to a classmate.

The Index